# TOUCH OF INNER POWER

Paramhansa Yogananda

# TOUCH OF INNER POWER

## LIVING THE TEACHINGS OF
### *Paramhansa Yogananda*

NAYASWAMI JYOTISH
AND NAYASWAMI DEVI

CRYSTAL CLARITY PUBLISHERS   Commerce, California

**CRYSTAL CLARITY PUBLISHERS**
1123 Goodrich Blvd. | Commerce, California
crystalclarity.com | 800.424.1055
clarity@crystalclarity.com

ISBN  978-1-56589-092-3 (print) | CIP  available
ISBN  978-1-56589-538-6 (e-book) | CIP  available
ISBN  978-1-56589-835-6 (audiobook)

Cover layout design by Tejindra Scott Tully
Interior layout by Michele Madhavi Molloy
Cover image by Freepik

The Joy Symbol is registered by
Ananda Church of Self-Realization
of Nevada County, California.

# CONTENTS

# ART AND PHOTO CREDITS

Most of the paintings you're about to enjoy in a number of these blogs were done by Nayaswami Jyotish. Included also are a couple of others by other Ananda artists. We list each painting here along with its page number and a link you can use to view it as a larger image and, if you'd like, to purchase it as a print. These are just a few of Jyotish's many paintings; you can see them all at **crystalclarity.com/111**.

# PHOTO CREDITS

We offer grateful appreciation to the many Ananda residents who over the years have contributed photographs to the Ananda Image Library. Almost all the photos in the book that aren't listed below were taken from that library. A handful of others are in the public domain.

| | |
|---|---|
| 7 | Pixabay |
| 29 | Pixabay |
| 37 | Pexels |
| 45 | Pixabay |
| 49 | Barbara Bingham |
| 55 | Pixabay |
| 22 | Nara Bedwell \| **crystalclarity.com/162** |
| 73 | Pixabay |
| 76 | Pixabay |
| 91 | Pixabay |
| 121 | Pixabay |

# PREFACE

L ife in today's world is challenging. The senseless hatred, violence, and divisiveness we see globally can leave us bewildered and without hope. But behind the clouds of darkness is an eternal light that, if we seek it, can bring us hope, understanding, and a better future.

In 2013 we began writing a weekly blog called "A Touch of Light," based on the teachings of our great guru, Paramhansa Yogananda. Our purpose was to give people a weekly message of inspiration to help them find meaning, strength, and guidance for the challenges in their daily life.

Eleven years have now passed since we began writing these blogs, and to our amazement the total number is now nearly six hundred separate installments. These have been published as five earlier books: *Touch of Light*, *Touch of Joy*, *Touch of Peace*, *Touch of Love*, and *Touch of Divine Wisdom*. Here now is the sixth in the series: *Touch of Inner Power*.

The world we find ourselves in today is even more stressful and confusing than when we began writing these blogs. That's why the theme of "inner power" is so important and relevant now. It does not signify power over others, so much, or over outer circumstances, as over ourselves: the ability to think, speak, and act in ways that are uplifting and strengthening to ourself and to those around us.

Within each of us lives an "inner warrior" that enables us to face challenges successfully. It's what gives us the power to persevere in spite of difficulties. Paramhansa Yogananda wrote: "Life is a struggle for joy all along the way. May I fight to win the battle on the very spot where I now am." This battle needs to be fought also with joy and the conviction that a greater power is fighting with us.

What motivates us to keep writing these blogs every week? In part, it's the regular notes of gratitude that we receive from the thousands of people worldwide who receive them. Here's a small but representative sample of comments that people send us:

"Thank you so much for this advice which is so full of hope."

"I love your messages that I get in my email! They are little nudges of encouragement and reminders for me. Thank you so much!"

"I cannot tell you how relevant this is to me right at this moment."

"Thank you for your inspiring words: just — as so often — what I needed to read and absorb today."

"Beautiful words and so pertinent to my life now. The article really touched me. Thank you."

So we offer you *Touch of Inner Power*. It's our hope that these "bolts of encouragement and strength" will help you fight your own battles. Read them; share them; live them. The eternal truths they contain can guide you forward to the divine light which shines within you and within every soul on earth.

NAYASWAMI JYOTISH
NAYASWAMI DEVI
Ananda World Brotherhood Village
February 13, 2024

# TOUCH

## of

# INNER POWER

# PRIORITIES

2022! We made it through 2021 and can look toward a new and (let's hope) better year. Now is a good time to review our goals and priorities for the year ahead.

Swami Kriyananda often told us this story: A very sincere devotee of God made a vow. "If ever You call me, Lord, I will drop everything and come to You." As the years passed, he married and took on modest worldly responsibilities. Then tragedy struck: His wife died in childbirth, and he was left alone with a newborn babe. It was at this most delicate hour that he heard God call, "Come to Me, My child."

He pleaded with God, "I will honor my vow and come to You, but I have a human heart, too. Please help me also fulfill my responsibility to my helpless child." And then he heard God respond: "Place your infant in a basket on the side of the road and hide behind a tree." Confused, but trusting, he did so.

Soon he heard the sound of horses and the murmurs of travelers. As he silently watched, the queen of the land and her entourage approached. Upon seeing the helpless baby in the basket, she stepped down from her carriage and took the babe in her arms. "What a lovely child," she said. "I will raise it as my own." Thus the devotee was able to fulfill both his vow to God and his worldly responsibilities.

This story is, of course, symbolic. And, as a symbol, it applies to each of us. What are the priorities, responsibilities, and habits that prevent us from answering God's call? What are we willing to offer, and what do we hold back? Few of us are ready to pass a challenge as severe as the devotee's in this story, but we each must face tests at our own level.

Most of us still have areas where our karma is not yet finished: Perhaps the ties that keep our souls from rising into the heavens are attachments to job, health, family, and relationships. They may even be the repeating entanglements of our "I'm right and they're wrong" conflicts.

"God's Boatman," by Nayaswami Jyotish.

But we must begin our journey somewhere. In the Bhagavad Gita Krishna says, "Whenever anyone, with pure intention, offers Me even a leaf, a flower, a piece of fruit, or water, I accept his offering." These two extremes — offering anything whatsoever, and giving absolutely everything — represent the length and breadth of the spiritual path.

If we are not able to renounce everything, there is a gentler approach, which was exemplified by Swami Kriyananda's mother. She asked God to help her in her motherly responsibilities and thus made them sacred. Swamiji writes in *The New Path*, "My mother told me that throughout her pregnancy she was filled with joy. 'Lord,' she prayed repeatedly, 'this first child I give to Thee.'"

God is always waiting for us to make an offering. Each time we sit to meditate, the Christ consciousness at the spiritual eye calls to us, asking us to transmute the ego into light. If we find that our mind is plagued by distractions, then let us lay our preoccupations beside the road and move away from the boisterous lanes of this world.

January 5 is Paramhansa Yogananda's birthday. He, like all great souls, had to make the journey of many lifetimes from giving nothing to giving everything. Having succeeded, he chose to incarnate in order to help set our feet on the path to our own destiny. In his poem, "God's Boatman," he said with love and compassion all but inconceivable to us:

> I want to ply my boat, many times,
> Across the gulf after death,
> And return to earth's shores
> From my home in space.
> I want to load my boat
> With all those waiting, thirsty ones
> Who have been left behind,
> That I may carry them to the opalescent pool
> Of iridescent joy,
> There where my Father distributes
> His all-desire-quenching, liquid peace.
> Oh! I will come back again and again!
> Crossing a million crags of suffering,
> With bleeding feet, I will come,
> If need be, a trillion times,
> As long as I know that
> One stray brother is left behind.

*In divine friendship,*
NAYASWAMI JYOTISH

# MIRACLE OF MIRACLES

After years of failed attempts to manifest my New Year's resolutions (ever happen to you?), I finally hit upon an approach that really does seem to work. When I shared this new strategy with friends at a recent satsang at Ananda Village, some of them asked me afterwards, "Could you write a blog about this so we can better remember it?" So, here it is.

Paramhansa Yogananda spoke often about the power of the mind to control our destiny. For many years as a young man he'd been plagued with chronic indigestion and was uncomfortably thin. Though he'd tried a great variety of remedies, his painful condition persisted.

Then came the day, Yoganandaji wrote in his autobiography, when his guru, Sri Yukteswar, fixed his gaze piercingly on him. "You are too thin," he declared. "Medicines have limitations; the creative life-force has none. Believe that: you shall be well and strong." Yoganandaji said his guru's conviction made such a strong impression on his mind that he was healed instantly, and permanently.

What factors were at play in this remarkable story? First there was the divine power of the God-attuned guru, Sri Yukteswar, but there was also the fertile soil of the disciple's receptive mind. Both are needed.

Master said, "The mind is the miracle of all miracles God has created." A strong mind with firm resolve has the power to break the chains of limitation and past karma that bind us. With this thought in mind, I began inwardly asking, "How can I use my mind to make the changes I want in my life?" Instead of focusing on the specific form or object I wanted to change ("I renounce doughnuts," for example), I realized I should think more about the process itself.

In other words, what is the operative factor in any beneficial change we are able to make? It is the innate power of the mind released to overcome the nay-saying, self-limiting ego. Thoughts like "You'll never be able to give up doughnuts" are swept aside like debris in a powerful current when the mind force is unleashed.

So for 2022 my resolution is this: "*I resolve to use the power of my mind to overcome all obstacles and accomplish my goals*." Remember the importance of attuning to the consciousness of a God-realized master. Let the Master's power infuse your mind to accomplish your goals. Then you can be sure your aims are for your highest good, and that you'll succeed.

Once we begin tapping into the unlimited power of the mind, there's another strategy we can use to confront any challenge. Looking ahead to the coming year, there are many potential causes for concern, and it's all too easy to fall into worry, anxiety, and fear. But we can use the disciplined mind to face whatever comes and look for God's presence there. Master said, "Link every state of mind with God."

You might think, "That's easy enough to do when things are going well." But using this technique, I've found even greater joy when I can bring God to mind in the difficult times as well: in the midst of challenges or discouragement. It's then we realize that

His divine joy is always accessible, even behind life's shadows. Swami Kriyananda put it this way: "There is a joy appropriate to every situation."

By aligning the miracle of our mind with higher consciousness we can use its power to build a better tomorrow, and to help all those around us.

I'll close with an excerpt from Master's prayer/demand, "Help Me to Win the Battle of Life":

"O King of Kings — train Thou in me, in the camp of discipline, the noble qualities of calmness and self-control. Protect the celestial kingdom of my mind against entry by the tenacious warriors of evil. Let Thy banner of peace wave always above the strong castle of my soul."

May Master's blessings be with you in the new year.

NAYASWAMI DEVI

# SECLUSION

L ast week Devi and I spent a period apart and in seclusion, the first time in several years that I had had a chance to be totally alone with God as my sole focus. It was wonderful!

My heart began to soar as even a few days of seclusion helped me realign my habits with my lifelong priorities. The world has its own pulls and magnetism. Even sincere devotees find a gradual dilution of their longing for spiritual liberation. Seclusion helps us reorient toward the subtler "gravitational" pull of God's love for us.

Paramhansa Yogananda said, "Always remember that seclusion is the price of greatness. In this tremendously busy life, unless you are by yourself, you can never succeed. Never, never, never. Walk in silence; go quietly; develop spiritually. We should not allow noise and sensory activities to ruin the ladder of our attention, because we are listening for the footsteps of God to come into our Temple."

I often chanted silently during the week, which helped to open the heart. One chant came spontaneously into my mind, and I later remembered that Swami Kriyananda writes about it in *The New Path*:

"During the Christmas meditation that year Master led us in singing his chant, 'Do not dry the ocean of my love, with the fires of my desires, with the fires of my restlessness.' Over and over we sang it. 'Christ is here,' he told us. 'Sing it to him.' Later he added, 'Because you have sung this chant here today, whenever in future you feel delusion pressing in upon you, sing it again, thinking of this occasion, and Christ and Guru will come down themselves to save you. Mark my words, for they are true.'" These words apply equally to us if we sing with devotion. God and Gurus are beyond time and space, and are eagerly awaiting those moments when we call to them with deep sincerity.

*"First Day of Spring," by Nayaswami Jyotish.*

There are three essential elements to seclusion. The first is **withdrawal** from outward activities. It is important to disengage from electronic devices with their incessant demands and lures. The second is to **focus** on God alone. During the week, when I wasn't meditating I read only from the books of Master and Swami Kriyananda. Finally, there is **feeling God's presence** as a constant. When our feelings, which are usually disturbed by daily events and demands, are allowed to calm themselves, we are much more able to hear God's whispers, and to feel Him close.

Swami Kriyananda said that one of the most blissful times in his life was four weeks he spent in seclusion in a holy cave, Vashishtha Guha, located on the banks of the Ganges above Rishikesh, India. (Although it was his karma to do a large and busy public work, he told those close to him that his natural inclination was to be a hermit.) He added, with a chuckle, that it was later discovered that a cobra had been living with him in that cave throughout his seclusion. Maybe it was Lord Shiva watching over him and adding his blessings to Swamiji's efforts!

Admittedly it is not easy for most people to find time for seclusion in their busy lives, although we should all make the effort. An interesting insight came to me this morning: Every meditation is a miniseclusion. The same three elements are needed: *withdrawal*, *focus*, and *feeling God's presence*. Without them meditation will be scattered and ineffective. These three seem to be like fundamental spiritual forces of nature, required in any successful spiritual search.

So, my friends, try to be alone with God and with your own higher Self. Take a seclusion whether it be for a month, a week, or an hour. You will find that it resets your priorities, opens your heart, and refreshes your soul.

*From the Inner Silence,*
NAYASWAMI JYOTISH

# OUT OF TIME

In last week's blog, Jyotish talked about some of the insights he received during his seclusion. Today I'd like to share with you also some that came to me during this time (or more accurately this "time out").

*I was "outside" of time and could simply rest in the present moment.*

As soon as I closed the door and entered the Crystal Hermitage Guest House, where I spent my seclusion, I was filled with a lovely sensation. Usually, as we deal with daily life, we feel our time is broken up into many discrete units, each with its own demands. There's the time to get up, to make breakfast, go to work, have meetings, answer emails, pick up the children, and on it goes. . . . And as we huff and puff our way through each day, we never seem to have enough time to get everything done — we simply "run out of time."

But knowing that I had no commitments for a week, I had the wonderful feeling as I began my seclusion that I had stepped "out of time" in a different sense of the words: I was "outside" of time and could simply rest in the present moment. It's surprising how rich that experience was.

The literal translation of the Sanskrit word "maya," or cosmic illusion, is "the measurer." It is the power that seemingly breaks up

Cosmic Unity into separate parts, creating divisions and limitations. Caught in the web of maya, we measure the minutes, hours, months, and years, and rarely have the opportunity to step back to experience time in a different way: as the Eternal Now.

In his poem "*Samadhi*," Master writes: "Present, past, future, no more for me, But ever-present, all-flowing I, I, everywhere." When we step "out of time," and loosen the grip of maya, we can experience ourself as a part of a great oneness with all life.

Try this experiment. When you awaken in the morning and as you're going to sleep at night, rest in the thought of timelessness. Your true reality is not what you do or have done, where you go or will go, but is eternal and unmoving. Watch your breath slow down, and enjoy this expansive feeling of "all-flowing I everywhere."

During seclusion I also worked towards longer, deeper meditations. To help with this, I began looking through Swami Kriyananda's little book of daily inspirations, *Secrets of Meditation*. The very first "secret" proved extremely useful: "The secret of meditation is relinquishing outward attachments, and affirming divine freedom within."

Swamiji chose his words well here: he didn't say "renouncing" or "denying" outward attachments, but "relinquishing" them. The nuanced meaning here is to *surrender* our attachments as an offering to God for his safekeeping. He will keep watch over all of the people, plans, and possessions in our life, and they'll be waiting for us when we finish our meditation. But for a brief period, we can put them "out of mind" and rest in the well-being and freedom of the inner Self.

You'll actually enjoy everything even more when you break the bonds of attachment, because in reality nothing is ours. Master expressed this thought beautifully in his poem "They Are Thine."

I have nothing to offer Thee,
For all things are Thine.
I grieve not that I cannot give;
For nothing is mine, for nothing is mine.
Here I lay at Thy feet
My life, my limbs, my thoughts and speech;
For they are Thine, for they are Thine.

So, here are two insights from my seclusion that may help you on your spiritual journey: Step "out of time" and put things "out of mind." It's been refreshing and inspiring to integrate these attitudes into daily life. Why not try them and see for yourself if you, too, experience more inner joy and freedom?

*With loving thoughts,*
NAYASWAMI DEVI

# WHAT GOES, WHAT STAYS

I n the last two months we have seen two great souls depart this world. Nayaswami Seva passed away on November 14th, and we just held an Astral Ascension Ceremony for Nayaswami Anandi, who passed away five days ago. Anandi had been a member of Ananda and our dear friend for more than fifty years. The talk given at the ceremony by her lifelong husband, Bharat, was particularly touching.

Yet, as all of us must do, these friends have moved on to the astral world. What remains? What is permanent? Memories may stay alive for a time, but only God's eternal qualities stand unchanged by the crashing waves of maya. I would like to look past Anandi's personality and touch on a few of the qualities that she manifested, in ways that were particularly inspiring to me:

*A lesson from Anandi: Mold your life around your search for God.*

**Everything was God-centered.** Anandi was very clear that the purpose of this life was to find spiritual liberation, and she shaped her life around that goal. She was always listening for God's whispers drawing us back to the bliss of our true Self. Though she held many different jobs and roles and gave countless classes and talks, she never identified herself with what she did.

We spent a lot of time working together with her, walking together, and connecting about little things in the way true friends do. She never judged people, nor had any tendency to get into negativity or gossip. I remember one walk where the conversation started to drift toward some problems and negative qualities of one of the guests. Anandi quickly said, "Let's talk about something more uplifting."

*A lesson from Anandi: Mold your life around your search for God.*

**Selflessness expressed by serving others.** There were hundreds of people whose lives were uplifted and changed by talking with her. She spent a lot of time talking with visitors, and never considered it as anything special. But they did! Her husband, Bharat, said that they received over a thousand notes of appreciation after her passing. She was extremely humble in the true sense of the word: not thinking about herself. Because of that, she was able to allow the space for people to feel safe enough to open up the deeper parts of themselves.

*A lesson from Anandi: Dissolve your ego through humbly serving others.*

**Persistence.** When Anandi took up a task, you knew that she would see it through to the end no matter what it took. As an example, she created the wonderful eight-book series, *Wisdom of Yogananda*, compilations of Master's teachings on various topics. Just think of the countless hours it must have taken to study, extract, and categorize those wonderful quotes.

*A lesson from Anandi: Stick with the job until it is done. And, your main job is yourself.*

*A lesson from Anandi: Live joyfully.*

**Joy and good humor.** The name, Anandi, that Swami Kriyananda gave her means "joy." And there was a stream of joy and good humor that flowed beneath the surface, always ready to well up in a laugh, a quick, amused comment, or a smile. Of all the things of value that Anandi shared with me, I think that her joy was the most important. It is the very essence of who she was, who we all are.

*A lesson from Anandi: Live joyfully.*

These are just a few of the many eternal qualities of God that Anandi manifested. And, while her body and personality may be gone, the examples from her life are forever woven into the fabric of Ananda. Soon we will have a memorial service where friends from around the world can share more stories. It is sure to be filled with God's light and joy. That is to say it will be filled with Anandi.

In joy,
NAYASWAMI JYOTISH

# A LIFE IN GOD

As a child, I hadn't the slightest thought that I would live my life for God, but that proved to be my destiny. For some people this concept of living for God might seem intimidating, or grim, or filled with dour self-sacrifice and denial. But it's quite the contrary. From my own experience and that of hundreds of others I know, such a life is filled with fulfillment and joy on all levels.

Why? Because God is the source of true happiness that will flow into our experiences if we break down the barriers we've built around our heart. When we place Him/Her at the center of our life, all of our activities are enriched by this mighty current of Divine Consciousness.

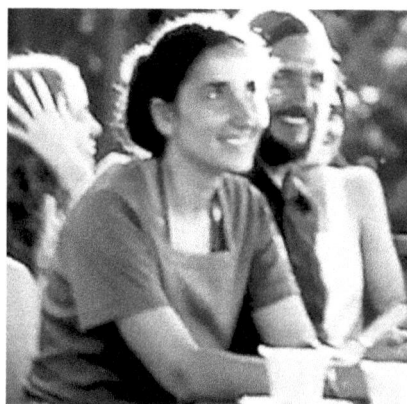

Here are a few of the ways that living for God is fulfilling:

### Achieving Our Goals

When, in meditation, we train our mind to concentrate, we can focus more effectively on whatever task is at hand. Turning our attention to a goal with focused, heightened energy helps us to persevere until we achieve it.

Once, a group of us joined Swami Kriyananda in painting his (then) new dome at Crystal Hermitage. Being around Swamiji's highly focused energy, we grew unaware of the passage of time, and painted nonstop for seven hours. Finally, at two in the morning, we realized we'd finished the job! On that occasion Swamiji showed us that we can accomplish any task when we forget about ourselves and focus on what we're doing.

## Finding Solutions to Our Problems

Often life seems like a never-ending series of problems — we fix one, only to have two more pop up. But living for God gives us not only strength and resilience, but a powerful, unseen partner to help us along the way. By tapping into a positive flow of energy, we can meet every obstacle with confidence that there *is* a solution.

In building Ananda, we've encountered countless challenges: forest fires, lawsuits, financial crises, to name a few. I remember a community meeting with Swamiji in July 1976, only a few days after the forest fire had burnt the community to the ground. Rallying the "troops," Swamiji led us all in a solution-oriented discussion about how we could earn money to rebuild, construct simple dwellings to get through the winter, and more. It all seemed very doable, and in fact it all was.

Positive thinking draws solutions. When we live in that spirit, then God also steps in and presents unexpected opportunities to support our efforts.

## Loving Others

People may have the misconception that a life in God means cutting oneself off from others, and becoming aloof or cold. It's not so! God is the source of all love. The more we love Him/Her, the more our love flows out to everyone and everything around us. Our relationships with our friends, family, partners, children, and coworkers all become deeper and more fulfilling.

Fifteen years ago Jyotish and I spoke at a yoga conference held in a large public park in Rome. The next day as we were strolling through the park, we passed a woman we'd never met who'd been at our talk. She immediately came up to us and said, "I have many troubles in my life. I felt so much love coming from you both. Can I write to you for support?" She's been in touch ever since, studied our teachings, and has taken Kriya initiation at our Assisi community. We've also watched her find peace and happiness in her life, and a growing ability to help others.

What happened was not about us, but about the power of God's love that can flow through each of us to change people's lives.

## Dealing with Change

Swami Kriyananda wrote, "The secret of earthly happiness is to flow gracefully with change. Allow things freely to come and go. All things pass: people, events, time — life itself. Learn to accept every fresh experience joyfully."

Everything around us will change, but we can train ourselves not to react with fear or sorrow, but to live with calmness and joy under all circumstances. As you may know, at Ananda Village we've had two dear friends pass away in the last three months. The way they approached their "final exam" was a powerful testament to the benefits of living for God. Whether by serving to the last moment of life, or by consciously releasing all attachments, they both exited with inner freedom and joy.

Though we feel a sense of loss at their passing, there is very little sorrow. Rather, there is a deep appreciation for the years of loving friendship we shared, and a quiet happiness for the soul freedom of our departed ones.

A saint once said, "Finding God is the end of all sorrow." When we live only for ourself, we are forever tossed about on the alternating waves of gain and loss, pleasure and pain. A life in God enables us to achieve our goals, solve our problems, love more deeply, and know a joy unaffected by any outward change. It's truly a life worth living.

*Your friend in God,*
NAYASWAMI DEVI

# CHALLENGES AND SOLUTIONS
# FOR OUR TIMES

W e are just finishing our annual winter program, Inner Renewal Week. During this event we try to make our classes deeper than usual and tailor them to more serious truth seekers. The theme for this year has been *Challenges and Solutions for Our Times*. A central focus has been that only through changes in consciousness can permanent transformation take place.

We began the week by looking at challenges and solutions for society at large. It is helpful first to assess world consciousness in terms of our present level of spiritual development. According to Sri Yukteswar, we have transitioned from the lowest age, Kali Yoga — the age of form and matter — and are currently in early ascending Dwapara Yuga, the age of energy. Consciousness now is beginning to advance, but society's overall level of maturity is still quite low. We have the increased energy that comes with Dwapara Yuga, but not yet the maturity to handle it responsibly.

In my opinion, the three biggest problems we face today are:

1) the polarization and tension between various political, religious, and national factions. Until people want to find common ground, neither solutions nor harmony can emerge.

2) a world still driven by greed. There is an increasing concentration of financial resources in a very small

group of people and businesses for whom profit is more important than the welfare of others. Their never-ending thirst to possess more than they do is widely shared by others, however less well placed many of them are to attain it for themselves.

3) the economic disruptions we will face in the near future as we try to prop up a teetering economy in a world in conflict on so many different levels.

Unfortunately, world peace and harmony cannot be achieved given the current immaturity of world consciousness, and will have to await the slow wheel of time. Since we cannot expect solutions to come from outside, we must look within. Our task is first to change ourselves, and then to share our uplifted awareness with all those willing to accept it.

Fortunately for us, God is on our side. Every little effort we make is met by His grace. When we are really ready to change, He will draw us to the guidance of a guru.

In this excerpt from his autobiography, Paramhansa Yogananda described his first meeting with his guru, Sri Yukteswar:

"O my own, you have come to me!" My guru uttered the words again and again in Bengali, his voice tremulous with joy. "How many years I have waited for you!"

His eyes held unfathomable tenderness. "I give you my unconditional love. Will you give me the same unconditional love?"

"I will love you eternally, Gurudeva."

Then, when Sri Yukteswar suggested that Yogananda return to his family in Calcutta, Yogananda balked. At this, Sri Yukteswar said, "The next time we meet, you will have to reawaken my interest: I won't accept you as a disciple easily. There must be complete surrender by obedience to my strict training."

Interestingly, when Swami Kriyananda met Yogananda and asked to become his disciple, a similar exchange took place. Swamiji wrote, "Gazing at me with deep love, he said, 'I give you my unconditional love. Will you give me your unconditional love?'" When Swami replied "Yes!" Yogananda continued, "And will you also give me your unconditional obedience?"

This, then, is the pattern we too must eventually follow. After a deep search for solutions, our hearts and minds will be ready for inner transformation. As God guides us back to Him, He will ask of us two things: unconditional love and unconditional obedience. Though our egos may resist, we must come to the point where we offer these of our own free will. It is then that the true inner transformation can begin to take place.

This morning in meditation I repeated over and over to Yogananda, "I give you my unconditional love and obedience. Please guide me to God, to my own true Self."

As I did so, I was filled with a deep sense of gratitude and joy, and the desire to serve as a channel of God's unconditional love to all.

*In the light,*
NAYASWAMI JYOTISH

24

# CHOOSE YOUR MEMORIES

When I was a young child, I would occasionally wake up crying in the middle of the night from a bad dream. Fortunately, I had a wise, loving mother who would come and sit by my bed to comfort me. Her advice on such occasions was always the same: She didn't ask about the scary dream, but would say, "Let's think about some happy memories, like when our family went to the ocean. Remember how much fun we had?"

Invariably, I would start feeling better, the scary dream would fade from memory, and I would soon drift back to sleep. Though I don't think that my mother was aware of it, she was sharing with me an important aspect of Paramhansa Yogananda's teachings: the right use of memory to change our consciousness.

He wrote: "Memory was given to us to keep alive only life's good experiences and lessons. Get rid of wrong thoughts by avoiding recalling them. If they come to mind in spite of you, refuse to entertain them. Let me repeat: To remember bad experiences and dwell upon them is an abuse of God's gift to us of memory."

For the past two years, we all have faced many challenges in dealing with the global pandemic. The signs are starting to seem hopeful that we may be moving past the devastation of Covid into a new era free of the suffering and loss that we've seen. These painful experiences have left deep impressions for most people which have the potential to influence their life into the future.

Now is an important time to work consciously with our memories so that we don't carry the suffering forward with us. Memory is the mental note made of every thought or action when it first occurs, which is stored in the brain as a thought pattern. The word "remember" comes from *re*, "again," and *memorari*, "to be mindful of."

Try consciously to bring to mind the good memories you've acquired during this period: the kindness of strangers, an inspiring story about the efforts of medical teams to help others, the times of deepened prayer and calling on God, the fulfillment found in simple pastimes, or loving conversations with friends, to name but a few.

*Choose to recall good memories.*

Yoganandaji said, "Deep, alert attention with feeling is the needle that cuts grooves in the record of your memory cells." This is true for both positive and negative memories. Since our memory is linked to past karma, by concentrating on good memories we can actually ameliorate and change negative karmic patterns.

Master went on to say, "One should not bring back any wrong thought and relive it, for then it will stay longer in the mind. Through the right use of memory, we can reproduce those experiences of our past lives that are beneficial for the increase of knowledge in this life."

Avoiding negative people and media is also important in redirecting our memories toward good experiences. Destructive words and downward-pulling conversations have the power to keep us focused on bad memories. These will prolong the suffering long after an adverse experience is over.

So remember, choose to recall good memories: not only from the past two years, but from your whole life. This isn't being in a state of denial, but rather choosing to be free of the experiences that have brought you suffering. A focus on positive past experiences leads to a happier future. As Master said, "If you keep your brain, your mind, your body filled with happy memories, the greatest good of all, God, will come and remain with you."

*In His love,*
NAYASWAMI DEVI

# 9

## PRAYERS FOR PEACE

T he world desperately needs our prayers and goodwill at this time. The extraordinary events taking place in the Ukraine and Russia, as well as around the world, are sending out waves of dark, disturbed energy. Each of us must do what we can to counterbalance this darkness with light.

Paramhansa Yogananda gave a strong warning to the world in 1939, when Europe was on the brink of a World War II. Among other things, he said:

> "Why do world suffering and misery arise? When people all over the earth are happy and prosperous they are in tune with God, and the entire vibrations of the earth in relation with the planets are harmonious. But as soon as one nation starts fighting with another, or selfish industrial gourmands try to devour all prosperity for themselves, it brings depression. And when depression starts in one place, it begins to spread everywhere, owing to the vibrations that travel through the ether."

> "World War I created wrong vibrations in Europe first, which then spread all over the earth, and where there was no war, influenza appeared. The agonies of the people who died in the world war created the subtle cause of the epidemic."

> "Ye nations of the world, beware! Use your patriotism to protect your own country, and do not get mixed up with any other nation that advocates aggression. All nations should unite to noncooperate in every way with those

nations that want to start wars of aggression."

"The politicians are blinded by their patriotism, selfishness, and love of fame. Disregarding the divine laws laid down by God and voiced by great saints, they are bringing an avalanche of miseries upon the nations of the earth."

The repeat of history is eerie. Yogananda might have been speaking today rather than over eighty years ago about aggression and pandemic. But implicit in his warning, if one looks deeper, lies a message also of hope and instruction. These times of conflict can be a springboard to higher awareness, if we see them as a warning to raise our consciousness. Don't wait for others to act. Let peace begin in your own mind, and let it spread to those around you in ever-widening circles.

If bad vibrations can cause disease and depression, then good vibrations can create health and prosperity. It is our responsibility to send out strong radiations of peace and goodwill to counteract and neutralize negative ones.

Each of us can pray for peace.

It is very good that the world has united in confronting this aggression primarily through economic and non-violent means as Yogananda suggested. But we, individually, must also strongly confront the darkness of these times.

Each of us can pray for peace, act as angels of mercy to everyone we meet, and fill our thoughts and relationships with peace and harmony. On a more subtle level, it helps to remember that this world is but a drama, created and acted by Divine Mother. Everything is made of consciousness. With our uplifted consciousness, attuned to God's higher laws, we can help strengthen the light so it can prevail.

We have many friends, wonderful people, in the Ukraine, Russia, and throughout Europe. The innocent people do not want war. Let us try to help them! Visualize our friends and the entire area being filled with subtle vibrations of goodwill and benevolence. Pray earnestly for God's higher vibrations of love and kindness to spread.

I am making a pledge to do my best to act throughout each day with peace and harmony, and to strongly radiate those vibrations to the whole planet. Will you join me?

*In the light,*
NAYASWAMI JYOTISH

# FROM THE ONE TO THE MANY

The date was March 7, 1952. Paramhansa Yogananda stood to address the large crowd gathered at the Biltmore Hotel in Los Angeles to honor India's Ambassador to the United States.

Swami Kriyananda, who was present at that event, described what happened next in his book, *The New Path*: "His [Yoganandaji's] brief talk was so sweet, so almost tender, that I think everyone present felt embraced in the gossamer net of his love. . . . Finally he read his beautiful poem, 'My India.' . . . He came to the last lines: 'Where Ganges, woods, Himalayan caves and men dream God. / I am hallowed; my body touched that sod!' 'Sod' became a long-drawn-out sigh."

Those were the last words Yoganandaji uttered in this lifetime. His body fell to the floor, and he entered *mahasamadhi*, a liberated soul's conscious exit from the body.

In celebrating the anniversary of Master's *mahasamadhi*, I began thinking about his words to Swamiji at their first meeting on Sept. 12, 1948: "I give you my unconditional love." These were the same words that Master's guru, Swami Sri Yukteswar, had said to him at their first meeting nearly forty years earlier. Perhaps these same words have been spoken by guru to disciple from time immemorial.

This gift of unconditional love is more than just a sentiment expressed by one individual to another. It imparts the power of divine love from the consciousness of the guru to that of the disciple, and with it comes the disciple's responsibility to share it with all.

As sincere followers of a great master, it's important to understand that this is our gift, too. Yoganandaji has given his unconditional love, not to a select few, but to all who are earnestly seeking God. We must, however, do more than just receive it — we need to share it with others. Given the tragic conditions in today's world, what greater service can we be rendering at this time?

After the bombing of the World Trade Center in New York on Sept. 11, 2001, Swami Kriyananda wrote a letter to the Ananda communities worldwide. He said, "Though I very much wanted to pray, this drama is so vastly complex that, lacking a clear focus, no prayer of mine, surely, could be very effective. Then I thought of the prayer attributed to Saint Francis of Assisi*: 'Lord, make me an instrument of Thy peace.' And I thought, What better prayer than this for such a time?

"Divine love is a force. . . . If we understand that by loving rightly it is God's love we express, He will be able, through us, to uplift the world's consciousness. For that is how He works: through instruments; very seldom directly."

Recently Jyotish and I took part in a very moving online satsang with Ananda members from both Russia and Ukraine. As people from both countries spoke of their suffering, confusion, and anguish, many of us were weeping. One man from Russia said that his mother was Ukrainian and his father Russian, and he was filled with inner turmoil seeing what people from both countries were enduring. Another woman, a Kriyaban living in

---

* The prayer was actually written not by St. Francis, but by William I ("the Conqueror") of England. (See crystalclarity.com/164.)

Kyiv, told of the extreme hardship and fear caused by the constant bombing of her city.

That day I began praying for the people of both countries, but I focused especially on this one Ukrainian woman as a symbol of everyone involved.

I suggest that you too, as you pray for a resolution of this conflict, also visualize one child frightened by the destruction of their home; or one mother grieving over the death of her soldier-son; or one anguished soul yearning for peace. Focus your prayers on one of them. By deeply tuning in to one individual, vibrationally you can reach the hearts of many.

The sacred gift of divine love that is given by the guru comes with the responsibility to share it with all, lest it wither and die. Part of its power is transmitted through prayer, but another part is given through the living examples of followers of our path.

Receive God's unconditional love, share it with others as fully as you're able, and live the teachings. In these ways, the power of divine love will expand out from you and me to reach many. Eventually it can uplift the consciousness of the whole world.

*Seeking the One Heart that beats in all breasts,*
NAYASWAMI DEVI

# LOOKING AHEAD BY LOOKING BACK

L ast evening Devi and I had a satsang with a group of younger members living at Ananda Village and were asked a very interesting question. "If you could have a conversation with yourself at age thirty, what advice would you offer him?" What a fascinating question! Here are a few things I might tell my younger self:

**Protect, nourish, and deepen your intention to find God.** The yearning for union with God is your most valuable possession. If you keep this strong, everything else will somehow fall into place. The flame of longing for the Divine has to be fed with the fuel of discipline, devotion, and good habits. But unless that longing is kept vibrant, nothing outward can make it burst into flame.

Attunement is more important than technique. Align your individual will with God and Guru's. This alone will keep you on track. Make and keep good spiritual friends who are also attuned. Looking back, I'm sure that I couldn't have made much progress trying to go it alone.

**Relationships are nurtured by friendship and kindness.** Give love freely and actively just as the sun gives light to plants. Advice is best given only if people ask, and then given softly and kindly. Judgment always backfires, hurting you even more than those you judge.

**It is all about consciousness.** Don't get confused into thinking that the tests in your life are about the tests themselves.

Challenges will come, must come, but only in order to give you a chance to work on your consciousness. When they come, don't forget why you've drawn them. It is never about the project, but always about what you can become by facing them.

*Devi and Jyotish in the early years of Ananda.*

We just finished talking with our dear friends Shurjo and Narayani, who are leading Ananda's work in Mumbai. They are in the midst of a huge project, creating a space where people can come and experience the uplifting vibrations of Ananda and Swami Kriyananda. Its outer form will be a café, but its purpose is to be an environment where the patrons can experience a little bit of the astral energy of Ananda. Narayani said that she is praying daily for protection: not from any tests the project may bring, but simply to keep from forgetting why they are doing it and for whom. It is all a manifestation of love and service to God and Gurus.

**Don't be too impatient.** Self-discovery is a long process. You'll have to find a balance between effort and acceptance. A marathon is a strenuous race that takes the right level of effort in order to get to the end. Neither sprinting nor stopping will get you there. So it is with a spiritual marathon.

How can you find the right balance? It's actually pretty simple. If you *feel* like you're trying hard, you are. The rest is about relaxation and endurance.

**Have faith, God and Guru love you.** This is the final piece of advice I would give my younger self. If you calm yourself, especially in meditation, you can feel in your heart the sweetest feeling of all — the reciprocal love between you and God.

So, my young self, these are some lessons I've learned by traveling the road that lies ahead of you. Now, as Steve Jobs would say as he was about to walk offstage at the end of a presentation, "Oh, one more thing." Then came the big reveal.

So, "one more thing." Be happy along the way. You have to travel the road ahead one way or another. The road is dark and stormy when you're grim but sunny and warm when you're happy. Be happy.

In joy,
NAYASWAMI JYOTISH

# RISING FROM THE ASHES

ts true origin is unclear. Some say it was from ancient Egypt, others from Greek mythology. But whatever its source, the phoenix — the immortal bird which rises anew from its own ashes — is a powerful symbol for us today.

Both literally and figuratively, the world does seem to be crumbling into ashes: literally, as the cities of Ukraine are being destroyed by warfare; and figuratively, with the continuing pain and loss caused by the pandemic. People everywhere, sensing a grim future, are gripped with feelings of helplessness and hopelessness.

Yet, as with the rising phoenix, there is also the possibility that this is a time of rebirth and hope for a better world. The teachings of India say that all of creation is a constant cycle of death and rebirth. Whether it be the soul's cycle of reincarnation, or the yuga cycles of rising and falling civilizations, behind it all is a movement of renewal and growth towards higher consciousness.

Each of us can help the phoenix rise from the ashes and emerge into a future filled with peace, prosperity, and well-being for all. Paramhansa Yogananda gave us four Tools of Wisdom to help build this future.

**Wisdom Tool #1: "The season of failure is the best time for planting the seeds of success."** Though prospects may seem bleak at present, look beneath what's happening on the surface. The barren soil is being cleared of the dying plants of old ways of thinking so that seeds of new consciousness can take root. What are these seeds? The understanding that life is constantly reborn; that success springs from failure; and that God's plan for all of us is rooted in love and meant to bring our highest happiness.

**Wisdom Tool #2: Every test we face is a test of our will power, and if we choose to use it, we always have the strength to be victorious.** Once we understand that every challenge comes for the sole purpose of awakening our soul power, the path to victory becomes relatively straightforward and simple. Yoganandaji offered this beautiful prayer: "I will welcome all tests because I know that within me is the intelligence to understand and the power to overcome." Don't focus on the details of each test, but see the flow of energy that will surmount it. The ability to succeed is inherent within us, if we use our God-given intelligence and will power.

**Wisdom Tool #3: "There are no obstacles, there are only opportunities."** Someone once said, "When God closes one door, He opens another, but it's hell in the hallway." Doors are closing behind us as old ways of living are dying, and we may feel uncertain as we stand in the hallway of the present without a clear way forward. But if we can trust that facing the obstacles confronting us is the next step in our unfoldment, then new doors of opportunities begin to open for our inner growth.

**Wisdom Tool #4: "Change yourself, and you have done your part in changing the world."** Are we helpless beings in the grips of mindless aggression and devastating disease? Not at all! Using Master's wisdom tools and spiritual techniques, we can do our part to change ourself. As each of us faces the world with determination, courage, and hope, we can help the phoenix take birth anew, rising with strength and glory from the ashes of the old. One person, or a small group of like-minded people, seeking higher consciousness can do more good for the world than millions lost in the grip of delusion.

Swami Kriyananda wrote an inspiring song, "A New Tomorrow," which ends with these words:

> Even so, all of us together
>    Can create a better land!
>
> Leave the past: A new tomorrow
>    Waits for all who understand.

*Joined with you in rising Spirit,*
NAYASWAMI DEVI

# A SPIRITUAL REPORT CARD

Divine Mother is a master magician. There is a trick that all magicians use: The obvious hides the hidden. A big movement attracts our attention while the real magic is happening behind the scenes. God hides His presence, entertaining us with the beauties and terrors of this world. He gives us challenges, but we rarely understand that the real test is happening behind the scene, in our consciousness.

What befalls us in life is not especially meaningful, but how we react to our challenges, and what we become because of them, is of vital importance. As Paramhansa Yogananda's most advanced woman disciple, Sister Gyanamata, said, "Lord, change no circumstance in my life. Change me."

In my last blog I said, "Challenges will come, must come, but only in order to give you a chance to work on your consciousness. When they come, don't forget why you've drawn them. It is never about the project, but always about what you can become by facing them."

Let us take, for example, the "Covid years," when everyone in the world faced difficult tests. To the question, "How did you do during Covid?" a typical answer might go something like this: "I did pretty well. No one in my family died, and I was able to keep working. The isolation part was hard, and the government restrictions really got under my skin." This is a good example of missing the point.

The devotee, who knows that this is a trick question, might answer more like this: "I did pretty well. I deepened my faith in God even though my uncle died. My heart stayed open and even expanded with compassion for those who were suffering, and I did everything I could to help others."

Swami Kriyananda called death "the final exam." When we leave this world, we take nothing material with us, only our consciousness with all of its qualities, tendencies, and unfulfilled desires. Think of all the tests you face in this life, even the most severe, as quizzes only, helping you prepare for your finals.

The question naturally arises, "How can we prepare now in order to pass this final exam?" In school we know the subjects, and get a grade from the teacher. But life doesn't seem to give us clear feedback. It would help to at least know what we will be graded on.

In each life, you may have signed up for one or more special classes, which you can identify by those issues that recur again and again. But there are also "required classes" that everyone must take.

There is a danger in offering a report card. In fact many progressive schools have dispensed with them altogether, because the students focus on getting a good grade rather than on the process of learning. So, our Spiritual Report Card gives only two grades, a plus or a minus. Did we make progress in these areas or did our consciousness contract?

Here, then, are some of the test questions: Think of it as a "cheat sheet," a way of knowing in advance what you will be asked when your "Spiritual Report Card" for this life is written.

**Your connection with God:** Did your desire to find God, along with your faith and devotion, grow stronger or weaker?

**Attunement to guides and Gurus:** Were you able to align your free will with that of the Gurus? Their only purpose in coming is to tutor us so we can live in accordance with divine law.

*"The Land Beyond My Dreams," by Nayaswami Jyotish.*

**Qualities of the heart:** Did your heart's energy expand or contract? When life tested you, did you think of others? Did you expand your love, friendship, support, and compassion to include everyone?

**Strength of mind and will:** Were you able to keep your mind positive and your will strong? Master said that every test is a test of will. And also that we will never get a test that is too hard for us.

**Dharma:** Finally, did you stay in alignment with dharma? (You can use Patanjali's yamas as a guide: non-violence, non-stealing, non-lying, non-sensuality, and non-greed.)

So, my friends, prepare well. See everything that comes as a loving lesson from your Divine Mother meant to help you pass your exams and merge into divine bliss. And remember that the process of learning is more important than the results. We have all the time in the world to pass our exams.

*In joy,*
NAYASWAMI JYOTISH

# LOOK FOR THE SKYLIGHT

My friend was apprehensive and not a little frightened as she entered the room to begin her first radiation treatment. She'd recently been diagnosed with cancer, but fortunately the doctors had been reassuring — telling her that it was readily treatable, and that she should expect a full recovery.

Still, as she and her husband waited for the treatment to begin, not knowing what to expect, they were praying for help to face what lay ahead. Then they saw a large whiteboard on the wall with encouraging notes from patients to help others going through the same treatment. It filled their hearts with joy as they read such reassuring words as:

"Being alive is a constant prayer. . . . Have faith in the process."

"You never realize how much the love you give others comes back to you until you have cancer."

"Sometimes strong has nothing to do with muscle."

"At the end of your rope? Look up!"

"And just like that — you graduate!"

Weeks have now passed, and my friend is doing very well. One of the statements, "At the end of your rope? Look up!" reminded me of a remarkable story from the life of Swami Kriyananda.

When Swamiji was a young monk of twenty-three, he was asked by his guru, Paramhansa Yogananda, to help with the editing of his just-completed commentaries on the Bhagavad Gita. The year was 1950. "A new scripture has been born!" Yogananda declared to him ecstatically. "Millions will find God through this book. Not just thousands — millions! I have seen it. I know!"

Swamiji read all one thousand five hundred pages that Master had written. As he later wrote about that experience: "Never in my life had I read anything so deep, and at the same time so beautiful and uplifting." Master worked with him for some time on the project, but circumstances intervened, and Swamiji wasn't able to complete it.

Years passed. Kriyananda no longer had access to the original manuscript, but he never forgot about the editing work his guru had asked him to do. Finally, as Swamiji entered his eightieth year in 2005, he realized that he was running out of time to finish the project in the years left to him. Praying for help, he asked Master how he could accomplish the task without a copy of the manuscript from which to work.

Then one night Swamiji had a dream. In it he heard Master's voice saying to him, "Don't overlook the possibility of a skylight." At first he was puzzled by these words, but as he raised his thoughts upward, a remarkable thing started to happen.

Verse by verse, he began to remember what Master had written in his commentaries fifty-six years earlier. Swamiji told us, "Master's thoughts poured effortlessly into my mind, helping me to fill page after page with deep insights and inspiration." He completed the six-hundred-page book, *The Essence of the Bhagavad Gita*, in just under two months; his subsequent editing required only one month more. Through the skylight of God's grace, everything he needed had flowed to him.

Now, as both individuals and global citizens of a troubled world, we face many challenges. Let's remember to "look for a skylight." We can do this by lifting our eyes and energy up to the seat of higher consciousness, the spiritual eye, where God dwells within each one of us. It is an act of will, of faith, and of strength. When we do so, we will draw the grace to face whatever lies ahead.

As King David declared in Psalm 121:

> I will lift up mine eyes unto the hills,
> From whence cometh my help.
> My help cometh from the Lord,
> Who made the heavens and the earth.

In life's challenges, may you always look upward.

NAYASWAMI DEVI

# FEELING OVERWHELMED?

M any friends have told us lately that they are feeling stressed and overwhelmed. They aren't alone. Some surveys peg the increase of anxiety in the general population at more than 25%. This is, of course, not a new problem. Paramhansa Yogananda addressed it in a 1927 article, "Nervousness: The World's Disease."

Master identified the main causes of nervousness as 1) long-continued overactivity, 2) excessive stimulation of the senses from physical overindulgence, and 3) mental overstimulation from chronic fear, anger, sorrow, hatred, jealousy, discontent, or similar harmful emotions.

He said, "Any violent or prolonged excitement disturbs the flow of life force through the nervous system. If you put a two-thousand-volt current through a fifty-watt lamp, it will burn out the lamp. In the same way, excessive stimulation burns the nerves, cutting off the supply of energy and upsetting the functioning of the nervous system.

'The most damaging emotions are anger and fear. (Worry is usually a fear that something undesirable will happen.) As soon as you are angry or afraid, you burn the nerves.

"Anger burns the nerves in the brain and causes poisons to be secreted throughout the body. Fear burns the nerves that supply the heart and can cause heart trouble. Feelings of timidity destroy the nerve endings."

Merely understanding the causes of anxiety will not, of course, cure us of feeling overwhelmed. Here is a four-step approach to help fix this problem.

**Step 1: Prioritize and Trim.** A main cause of overwhelm is taking on too much. The first step is to separate that which we *must* do from that which we merely *choose* to do. Make a list of the demands in your life and separate them into these two categories. As you do this be sure also to consult the feelings of your heart and the whispers of your soul.

Swami Kriyananda addressed this in a satsang with Ananda Village members in 1990. He said, "A principle I try very hard to live by is to give from strength, not from weakness or exhaustion. I simply ignore demands if I'm forced to work in a way that makes me lose my peace. It's important to be with God, to meditate, to take time to be with friends. It's important to work from your center and not to overextend. Too much extension becomes tension."

He added, "Sometimes there are start-up periods and crises that demand extraordinary efforts. I'm saying: Don't make it a habit. Respect your rhythms."

**Step 2: Release Your Resistance.** A second major problem is the internal friction that comes from resisting that which we need to do. If you've followed the first step you should now have a two-part list. Try to eliminate some demands that aren't crucial. Determine to accept unavoidable duties willingly, even cheerfully. Negative reactions cause internal stress. Focus on the positive features of your responsibilities and you will soon see them grow easier. Above all, don't allow resentment and anger to fill your mind with poison. As Master said, "It burns the nerves in the brain."

**Step 3: Strengthen Yourself.** Your first responsibility is YOU. Take care of yourself so that you can take care of others. Remember, you have a body, a mind, and a soul, and each needs attention.

For the body: eat well, exercise daily, and get enough rest. But don't overdo any of these. For the mind, make time for some uplifting stimulation, deep thinking, and a little laughter. For your emotions, set aside time for those things and people that make you happy, and avoid things that make you upset or angry. In today's media-driven world this is a global problem, and it is burning up the world's nervous system. For the soul, meditate and serve others.

"Out of the Mist," by Nayaswami Jyotish.

**Step 4: Give Your Problems to God.** This may come as a shock to you, but you aren't responsible for the world's welfare. It is enough to take responsibility for your own well-being and to try to help those who are in your circle of influence. Leave the rest to God. In fact, here is an even better idea: Leave everything to God.

*With love,*

NAYASWAMI JYOTISH

# A RESURRECTION OF TULIPS

I've always enjoyed the beauty and poetry of words. There's a certain category that I find especially delightful: the terms for gatherings in nature. Expressions like "a flamboyance of flamingoes," "a murmuring of magpies," or my favorite, "an exaltation of skylarks," all hint at the glory of God's creation.

Well, I'd like to create one of my own now: a resurrection of tulips. Why resurrection? Yoganandaji describes the word in this way: "Resurrection means any beneficial change that happens to an object or to a human being. . . . You cannot sit still spiritually because you must either go backward or forward. Isn't that a marvelous truth that in this life you cannot remain stationary? Either you must accept changes which are harmful to yourself, or focus on those that are beneficial."

*Tulips in blossom this year. Photo by Barbara Bingham.*

Why tulips? Throughout the month of April Crystal Hermitage Gardens are open to the public to enjoy the beauty of 17,000 glorious tulips blooming in a wide variety of colors, shapes, and sizes. If you've ever planted a tulip, you know that the bulbs are not very exciting, having the appearance of a small onion. But put them in the soil in October or November, let the winter rains and snows keep them moist, and when April comes they more than fulfill their promise of beauty.

It isn't only the tulips that are resurrected, however. The ten thousand visitors who come to enjoy the gardens are also beneficially transformed. Coming from all over California, with a great diversity of young and old, of races and ethnic backgrounds, singly or in groups — all are "resurrected" by the beauty and harmony they find here.

*The chapel at Crystal Hermitage.*

It was Swami Kriyananda's dream to create "world-class gardens" at Crystal Hermitage, his home at Ananda Village. After visiting the tulip fields in Holland, he had the inspiration to recreate their beauty here in the Sierra Nevada foothills. Now this dream is a reality.

Swamiji, whose anniversary of passing, his "Moksha Day," is celebrated on April 21, would be delighted to see the thousands of people transformed by the beauty of these gardens. The joy on their faces and the laughter on their lips reflect their awakened understanding that behind all of life's challenges are God's loveliness and eternal peace.

Swamiji loved to share beauty with others, and wrote in his book, *Cities of Light: A New Vision for the Future*, "To draw God's light down to earth, pure hearts are needed — devotees whose will is to live in light. Even as squalor attracts negative energies, however, so outward harmony and beauty attract Godly energies. Man cannot create heaven on this earth, for heaven is in God. But his duty is to *reflect* heaven in all he does, and in all that he creates."

This work of reflecting heaven to others extends far beyond beautiful gardens. One of the teachers at Ananda Seattle's temple wrote us, "We have a weekly meditation group here, and recently we took it from online-only to hybrid in the Temple. Three weeks in a row somebody new joined in person. The first week, the new person came in and started crying right away because she had been holding herself together throughout the pandemic, losing her husband to cancer, and being diagnosed with cancer herself. Coming into the Temple sanctuary as she heard us praying, she said she finally could relax and feel safe once more.

"The next week another new person started crying after class, saying she hadn't known a place like Ananda existed, and her heart felt so touched and moved. And last week someone new came and didn't cry at all! Well, not so fast — the next morning I woke up to an email from her expressing gratitude that the meditation had helped her to regain her 'peace and silence in the realm of reconnecting with her heart.' She shared that she was crying, because her heart was so moved and grateful. If nothing else, we make people cry here. I say that tongue in cheek, of course."

So, my friends, I hope that your heart is as touched as mine in hearing how the divine gifts of beauty, prayer, meditation, and silence can transform the lives of others. "A resurrection of tulips" is a metaphor for the power of God to change all of life beneficially and fill it with His love and joy.

*In divine friendship,*
NAYASWAMI DEVI

# LEARN TO SQUINT

Squinting is an invaluable technique used by artists, and something we can apply in our own lives too. For artists, it's simple to do: you just periodically look at your work with your eyes partially closed. Here is what a very fine artist, Robert Genn, has to say about the subject:

"Looking at work with half-closed eyes has several benefits. Simply put, squinting makes note of weak areas. Squinting tells you what's wrong and what's bad. Squinting lets you know where darkness or lightness might be added. Also, by drawing together the eyelids, you see the subject as more or less reduced to black and white. When work is viewed without the benefit of color, decisions can be more readily made. It seems that in standard easel-working vision, you 'can't see the forest for the trees.'"

*Lahiri Mahasaya seated in lotus pose.*

Isn't that one of the common mistakes we make in life, focusing on the trees instead of the forest? If we apply the squinting technique to our lives, it will help us extract ourselves from all the details and see our major energy patterns. Doing this as a regular habit can help keep our lives on course.

Even the position of the eyes is significant. Here is what Paramhansa Yogananda writes about the great yogi, Lahiri Mahasaya: "His intense joy of God-communion is slightly revealed in a somewhat enigmatic smile. His eyes, half open to denote a nominal direction on the outer world, are half closed also. Completely oblivious to the poor lures of the earth, he was fully awake at all times to the spiritual problems of seekers who approached for his bounty."

How can we translate the physical squint of an artist into the mental and spiritual squint that would be so helpful in life? What is needed above all is to back off from involvement in the innumerable details and problems of daily living. Another way of describing a spiritual squint would be to look at the canvas of life through a mind that is half involved and half detached. See the broader goals of your incarnation: Are they poorly focused, or set off to the side? When our minds are too involved in problems or too focused on "the poor lures of the earth," we can't see the larger picture.

The best time for a spiritual squint is toward the end of a meditation, when our minds and hearts are already somewhat withdrawn. Relax your gaze up toward the point between the eyebrows and spend a few minutes considering the broad patterns of your life. Do they line up with your aspirations, or have you allowed your soul to get caught in a cobweb of little hopes, dreams, and worries?

Once you perceive the "weak areas and what's wrong or bad" it is time to get to work. Paint over those parts that should be eliminated and start adding more light and color to those parts that will bring you true joy.

Swami Kriyananda said, "We are all works in progress. God isn't finished with us yet."

With a squint and a half smile,
NAYASWAMI JYOTISH

# ARE YOU MAKING SPIRITUAL PROGRESS?

There's a story of a young disciple who came to his guru's forest ashram for training. The guru blessed him and asked him to begin collecting firewood for the ashram's stoves. Willingly he carried out this task, and as the days, months, and then years passed, he continued to serve humbly in this way.

One day as he was returning to the ashram with his load of wood, he tripped on a tree root, and a stick fell from his arms. As it dropped, it pulled out a few strands of his hair. Staring in amazement at the gray strands entangled in the piece of wood, he thought, "I came here as a young man, and now I am old with gray hair. I've wasted my whole life in carrying wood while other disciples have studied with the guru. I haven't progressed toward my goal of finding God." His eyes began to fill with tears.

Just at that moment his guru came running to him and caught his tears. "Don't you know," the sage said, "that if the tears of a soul as great as you touch the ground there will be famine in the land for seven years?" The guru then touched his forehead, and the disciple entered into union with God.

This beautiful story illustrates the point that it's very difficult to tell for oneself whether or not we're making spiritual progress. Are there any ways to know if our spiritual efforts are bearing fruit? Here are some signs to help guide you:

**Do you have greater understanding and compassion for others?** With spiritual growth, our consciousness expands so that we feel more keenly the joys and sorrows of others. With this heightened awareness comes a sense of connection and unity, and a strengthened desire to help others out of their suffering.

**Are you finding new perspectives on life that are bigger than your own likes and dislikes?** As the self-limiting confines of ego begin to dissolve, we get a broader view of life that embraces others' realities as much as our own. Swamiji defined maturity as "the ability to relate appropriately to other realities than one's own."

**Are you able more easily to accept people or situations that once used to bother you?** Are you beginning to wonder why a particular situation ever troubled you? With inner growth comes freedom from old karma that has kept us bound. Sister Gyanamata, Yoganandaji's most advanced woman disciple, loved these words from a chant: "Before my eyes / My dead self lies. / Oh bliss beyond compare!"

**Are you seeing new things in yourself that need to change?** This may seem contradictory to spiritual growth, but Swami Kriyananda once said, "If you see a flaw in yourself that needs correcting, don't despair, but rejoice. The flaw has always been there, but now that you finally see it, you can get to work on it."

**Are you able to remain "even-minded and cheerful" in all circumstances?** As an undercurrent of joy begins to permeate your consciousness, you'll realize that no matter what happens in life, nothing can touch that joy. A saint once said, "Joy is the infallible sign of the presence of God."

But I should also mention that there are some attitudes that are deterrents to our inner development:

**Don't keep looking for signs of spiritual progress.** Yoganandaji said that our spiritual efforts are like planting seeds. If you keep digging them up to see if they've sprouted, you only slow down their growth. Be a good gardener who lovingly cares for his plants, but has the patience to let them grow at their own pace.

**Remember that God is the Doer, and give your inner development into His hands.** In self-forgetfulness we are able to allow divine grace to transform us in ways we can't yet understand. With faith in God, over time we can achieve the goals we are seeking.

Once we were riding in a car with Swami Kriyananda, and he was commenting on the spiritual growth of various Ananda members. Quietly from the back seat I said, "I don't know that I've made much progress." With intensity Swamiji replied, "How can you say that? You're an entirely different person than when you came!" I'd been at Ananda for about fifteen years at that time, and I surely wasn't aware of the changes to which he was referring.

If our spiritual progress happens in ways that are difficult for us to see, we might be inclined to ask, "Who are we becoming through this process?" It may seem hard to define, but it's actually quite simple — the last two lines of Yoganandaji's poem, "*Samadhi*," say it all:

> A tiny bubble of laughter, I
> Am become the Sea of Mirth Itself.

In their own good time all of our efforts end in the endlessness of God's Ocean of Joy.

*Towards that Joy,*
NAYASWAMI DEVI

# LEVITY

A friend who is an architect and engineer made an amusing comment about Ananda that has always stayed with me. He said, "We engineers study the effects of gravity. We need to know how to keep structures from collapsing. But at Ananda it is the opposite: You study the effects of levity."

Levity, in this sense, is far different from the normal definition of humor or frivolity. In its deeper sense, levity is the flow of energy toward the bliss of our soul nature. Levity can even become levitation if the flow is strong enough. As Swami Kriyananda wrote in *Demystifying Patanjali*, Sutra 3-40, "By mastery over *udana* — the current within the deep spine which raises Kundalini through the sushumna to the brain — one gains the power of levitation, and of leaving the body at will."

Few of us need to concern ourselves with levitation yet, but we all should practice levity. How can we "in-joy" ourselves? Keeping in mind that the flow of energy needs to be elevating and expanding, I thought it would be fun to share how Swami Kriyananda enjoyed himself. Since May 19 is the anniversary of his birthday, let's start there.

Swamiji was attracted to both refinement and joy in many forms. One of these was good food. He

*A rainbow appears in Seattle, on the anniversary of Swami Kriyananda's moksha this past April.*

often invited a small group of friends to breakfast on his birthday. Many times breakfast consisted of "fun foods": pancakes, a wonderful fruit salad, fresh juice, and tea or coffee. Mainly what I remember though is the friendship, laughter, and delightful stories. Later in the day he might have a community gathering in the gardens around his home. Again, laughter and joy: the squeals of children playing in the pool, the aroma of food cooking on a grill, the murmur of small groups of people talking together. There was always music involved and often a play or skit. Occasionally, Swami would read a story from his favorite humorist, P.G. Wodehouse, sometimes laughing so hard he could barely finish a sentence. An amazing thing is that Divine Mother almost always attended these events dressed up in the form of a rainbow. On more than one occasion a rainbow appeared in a nearly cloudless sky as what is called a "glory."

Swami was focused in whatever he did — he had to be energetic and concentrated in order to produce so many books, songs, and talks. But some of our most enchanting memories are of the trips of celebration that he would take after finishing a big project. We often accompanied him and a small group to Carmel-by-the-Sea, a charming California coastal town that started out as an artist colony.

Carmel is very refined, as close as Swami could get to the European feel of his youth. After meditation we would usually stroll along the streets visiting small shops, or art galleries, or "Conway of Asia," a store that specialized in Asian and Indian antiques. We weren't so much interested in buying things as in enjoying the refined ambience. The highlight of the day was lunch or dinner at one of Carmel's many wonderful restaurants.

The main point here is that, in spite of his intense schedule, Swamiji always made time for uplifting enjoyment — for levity. And, as was his nature, he liked to share his joy with others. We would do well to take this as a model for our own lives. Set aside time for friends, for good meals, for laughter and song. It is all a part of the life of a yogi.

"Ever-new, ever-expanding joy" is the final goal of the spiritual path. It would be a shame to wait, to spend a lifetime being pulled down by the gravity of problems and world events. Let's find ways to practice levity. Swamiji did.

*In joy,*
NAYASWAMI JYOTISH

# DYNAMIC HARMONY

Recently we had a wonderful satsang with Nayaswamis Devarshi and Dhyana, who shared many inspiring stories about the work in Ananda India. Devarshi is the head of a small but growing monastery near Chandigarh in northern India. In talking about what's making their life together so uplifting, he spoke of their "dynamic harmony": a shared spirit of joy, service, and dedication.

Through this unifying energy, they've created a magnetic vortex that's drawing to them the wherewithal to accomplish amazing things. A handful of monks are sharing Yoganandaji's teachings with thousands of others throughout the world — and changing their lives. This spirit of dynamic harmony, Devarshi added, is helping the monks create an environment in which they too are growing spiritually.

What is this kind of harmony, and how can we develop it in our own life? It is not a passive state, but **an active, conscious way of being with others** — be they marriage partners, family members, friends, or co-workers. It begins by fostering a sense of **mutual trust** in which we offer unconditional support to others under all circumstances. Then we must strive to see the highest potential in others so that they feel our **sincere respect** for them.

By **sensitively listening** to those around us, we can know them better and develop a "common language" that leads to mutual understanding. **Shared higher aspirations and goals** are also important parts of this kind of harmony, because through them we build "bridges of light" that unite us.

When we develop this kind of harmony with others, several things happen. If it's a working group, new ideas emerge and much more is accomplished. If it's a family group, problems are more easily resolved and a deeper love begins to blossom.

Swami Kriyananda spoke frequently about the need for harmony in our spiritual search. There was a woman in the early years of Ananda Village who had a hard time getting along with others. Once, after a big blowup with someone, she came to Swamiji in tears and asked, "Why can't I get along with people? Am I not in tune?"

He replied simply: "Attunement is harmony." In other words, living in harmony with others leads to deeper attunement with God. The woman began working with this concept, and her life improved.

Swamiji also said that living in community is like being in a rock tumbler. Into it go unpolished stones, whose rough contours he likened to our own, so long as our consciousness is of egoic separateness from others. The stones bump and tumble against one another, until in the end they come out shiny and polished, with beautiful shapes and colors. This process of smoothing out our rough edges isn't easy for any of us, but it helps us to achieve a spirit of harmony and unity which is a great boon on the spiritual path.

Swami Kriyananda, whose birth date we celebrate on May 19, was a wonderful example of how to live in dynamic harmony. Every book he wrote, every piece of music he composed was filled with an underlying spirit of harmony. The clothes he wore, the home he lived in, his voice, the way he walked — all reflected a harmony born of deep meditation and attunement with his guru.

In the way he related to others, Swamiji made everyone around him feel that they were an important part of his life and work. And yet, he was basically impersonal. His expanded awareness enabled him to feel a harmony with everyone he met, with all people, all life.

I'll close with this prayer-demand of Paramhansa Yogananda, which reflects the true source of dynamic harmony:

"Love is our souls' birthright! We demand, now, that all the rivers of our cravings be redirected through valleys of humility, eager self-sacrifice, and concern for others until, reinforced by Thy torrential blessings, they merge in the ocean of all fulfillment in Thee."

*With gratitude to those who have shown us the way,*
NAYASWAMI DEVI

# A STEP AT A TIME

W hy does it take so long, we wonder? It is common to experience a sense of frustration with our spiritual efforts. When progress seems to take forever, our very impatience can become an obstacle. We need to respect the way nature works and take things a step at a time.

A good friend, Sagar, shared this story from ancient India. But, first, a disclaimer: Warfare is a terrible solution for resolving conflicts in this world, as we are currently seeing with the tragic events in Ukraine. But as Yogananda pointed out in his explanation of the Bhagavad Gita, war can also be seen as a symbol of the inner struggle between the ego and the soul. So, let's take this story as a spiritual analogy.

Chanakya, a great general, undertook a noble war on behalf of his king. His first move was to attack the enemy's capital. This stronghold, however, was too well guarded. His forces were badly defeated, his army was scattered, and he had to flee into the wilderness.

One day, Chanakya entered a little village in quest of food. As he passed by a hut, he heard the excited voices of children. Their mother was serving them hot rice porridge. Suddenly a young boy cried out, "Ouch! I burnt my fingers."

"Well, what do you expect?" the woman said. "Naturally they will get burnt if you are as foolish as Chanakya." Intrigued and curious, Chanakya barged into the room.

"Who are you?" asked the mother of the children. "What do you want?"

"I just came in to find out the meaning of your words," said Chanakya.

The woman was surprised. "I was merely telling the children to eat properly," she said. "I had served them hot porridge. They should have realized that it was hottest at the center and started eating from the outer portion, which cools first."

"Yes, but what has Chanakya got to do with it?" asked Chanakya.

"Everything," said the woman smiling. "Chanakya was foolish to attack his enemy's strongest point, the well-guarded capital, at the very outset. Just like this silly child trying to eat the hot porridge from the middle! That's why Chanakya lost and had to flee. Instead, he should have started by first conquering the small provinces on the periphery in order to weaken it."

"Thank you so much, Mother," said Chanakya to the woman. "You've taught me a wonderful lesson in war strategy. I shall not make the same mistake a second time."

Chanakya regathered his troops for another attack. And this time the army set about conquering the smaller fiefdoms first. Advancing slowly but surely, they eventually succeeded in taking the capital.

"Going Within," by Nara Bedwell.

The lesson for us is that we need to take one step at a time, and win the small spiritual battles first before going on to the bigger ones. Take, for example, restless thoughts during meditation. We will end up frustrated if we assume we can quickly tame the mind. Let's conquer the outer provinces first. Start with the body, by keeping it relaxed and motionless. Then go on to the breath, just watching it come in and out without trying to control it. Try to practice *Hong-Sau* for a minute at a time with good concentration. Once you've achieved that, you will find it easier to focus on subtler aspects such as the inner sounds and lights. Work with achievable goals and celebrate the little victories. Over time you will naturally extend and deepen your concentration. Gradual growth is nature's way.

The same principle applies to other aspirations. In seeking to master your desires, for example, don't assume you can start with strongly defended, primeval ones such as security and sexual attraction. Work on manageable habits, taking on one at a time until you can transform it. Slow down in order to speed up. In the end, little steps lead to big results.

*With patience,*
NAYASWAMI JYOTISH

# WHEN THE BUBBLE BURSTS

'**ve** always enjoyed the pastime of blowing bubbles. Whether doing it as a child, or as an adult watching children delighting in it, the sight of iridescent bubbles floating through the air has never ceased to thrill me. I even had a friend who could blow different-colored ones on request: By some secret technique, pink, blue, or yellow bubbles would emerge from his wand.

The basic process is magically simple. You dip your wand into a soapy solution, blow gently through the hole, and voilà! The shimmering spheres emerge and dance before your eyes. Some bubbles last for only a few seconds, some come out in groups, some grow very large, and some, caught by a gust of wind, float high into the sky.

Paramhansa Yogananda used the imagery of bubbles in several of his chants and poems. One of my favorites is "Make Me the Sea":

> So do Thou, my Lord —
> Thou and I, never apart;
> Wave of the sea,
> Dissolve in the sea!
> I am the bubble;
> Make me the sea!

Drawing from Master's imagery, let's consider the soul's journey in terms of the life of a bubble. Just as we create them by dipping our wand into a soapy solution and then filling them with our breath, God creates our material body from His own iridescent consciousness, then enlivens it with life force, or *prana*.

Like the bubbles, some souls remain in their bodily form for but a brief period of time; some emerge in family clusters or spiritual groups; some have a bigger role to play; and some float high into the skies of divine consciousness. Whatever its particular journey, each individual bubble or soul must in the end merge back into the vast ocean of Spirit from which it came. For devotees, the desire to burst the confines of our earthly existence and merge back into the sea of Spirit is one of the strongest motivations on the spiritual path.

Will this loss of a separate existence be cause for sadness or regret? Not at all! When we become one with God, Swami Kriyananda explained, "it is not that we lose all identity; rather, we expand our identity to infinity. Being omniscient, . . . we retain the memory of having been, each one of us, a separate ego. In this way, Yogananda explained, nothing is lost in the Infinite — not even the ego. We can revive that memory of individual existence again, if ever the Divine wills that we return to earth to uplift and save other wandering souls."

When difficult events bear down and you feel discouraged or anxious, remember that the little bubble of your life is never separate from God's endless joy, peace, and love. You are a single drop of a much greater reality: an endless ocean of divine bliss. Master ends his magnificent poem "*Samadhi*" with these words:

> Gone forever, fitful, flickering shadows of mortal
> memory.
> Spotless is my mental sky, below, ahead, and high
> above.

Eternity and I, one united ray.
A tiny bubble of laughter, I
Am become the Sea of Mirth Itself.

*With bursting joy,*
NAYASWAMI DEVI

# SEE NO EVIL

S ee no evil, hear no evil, speak no evil. Most of us have seen the image of three monkeys, one covering his eyes, the next closing his ears, and the third one with his hands over his mouth. This ancient teaching suggests a wisdom that can really improve our lives if we put it into practice.

Paramhansa Yogananda guided the souls of his disciples on a subtle plane. Swami Kriyananda, in his book *Conversations with Yogananda,* quotes him as having said, "I go through your souls every day. I seldom tell what I see, though, because those things are sacred." Kriyananda continues, "The Master worked especially on raising our consciousness *from within*, if we were receptive to his vibrations, by helping us to change the direction of our thoughts and feelings. As someone once heard him say, 'If you shut me out, how can I come in?'"

I like to think that he is doing the same today for those of us who have opened ourselves to him.

Here is a sweet story of another instance of helping someone to change:

One sunny afternoon a man was strolling through a park, when he saw an old man sitting on a bench enjoying a cup of tea. Tentatively, he asked, "Dr. Allen, is that you?"

"Yes," the older gentleman replied, "and who might you be?"

"I was a student in your science class, and one day you did something that completely changed my life. You must remember me even though it was many years ago."

"I'm sorry, I don't recall your face. Can you refresh my memory?"

"I was young, poor, and foolish. One day while in class I stole my friend's watch. When he discovered it was missing, he went to you for help. You announced that no one could leave the classroom until the watch was found. Then you asked all the students to stand up and close their eyes, while you searched their pockets. After a time, you announced that the watch had been found and that everyone was free to go. What inspired me was that you let me leave without ever saying anything. From that time on, I made a vow to live a good life. Now, because of you, I am a teacher, too."

The old man smiled sweetly and said, "Oh, I remember the incident very clearly, but I don't remember you as the culprit."

"How is that possible?" asked the younger man.

"Well, you see, while I searched for the watch, I also kept *my* eyes closed."

All parents know the value of occasionally ignoring mistakes — turning a blind eye — when their children make some minor error in judgment. If human parents use this strategy, don't you think our spiritual parents, our Heavenly Father and Divine Mother, do too? And shouldn't we too, then, do the same?

It isn't as if we should be ignorant, or in denial about the mistakes we see around us. In fact, we should actively try to correct them. But, as we do so, let's be like that wise teacher. Let's help the situation without demeaning the person. People grow stronger when they are supported, not when they are condemned or punished.

For devotees, there should be a second image of those three

monkeys, one with their eyes, ears, and mouth open. And the caption should read, "See only goodness, hear only sweetness, speak only kindness."

*With goodness, sweetness, and kindness,*
NAYASWAMI JYOTISH

# THERE IS NO BAD KARMA

The old woman lay in bed critically ill and in great pain. For her daughter, who was providing loving care, seeing her mother's physical suffering was hard to bear. Even more difficult, though, was seeing her mental anguish. She kept repeating: "I must have very bad karma to be in such pain. God must be very displeased with me."

Seeking guidance, the daughter asked a friend of ours what she could say to comfort her mother. He wrote back: "Tell her there is no bad karma. There is only good karma, because everything comes to take us towards God."

When she read the letter to her mother, the old woman said, "Is that so? Then it's all okay. I'll keep that in mind at all times." Those few reassuring words made a huge difference for her. She was able to remain tranquil despite her suffering, and shortly afterwards, she peacefully left her body.

When adverse circumstances come, we may feel overwhelmed or even defeated by the thought that we're being punished through our bad karma. Remember that there are two related principles that God has put into play to help us move towards freedom: Free Will and the Law of Karma.

With free will, everyone has the ability to make choices about their life: which actions to take, what values to express, or what goals for which to strive. Free will is God's gift to help expand our awareness, but this gift is not without its price. The tuition we pay for making our own choices in the School of Life is governed by the law of karma.

Every action we take leaves an impression in our consciousness, which draws back to us exactly the kind of energy we've put forth. This reciprocal response of karma is not given in punishment or judgment, but is simply the mechanism through which we can continue our journey toward greater understanding.

In reality, there is no bad karma, but only the process of learning from our actions and adjusting them to bring greater happiness. This doesn't mean that we can avoid suffering if we've lived out of attunement with God's laws, but neither should we think of "bad" karma as a condemnation.

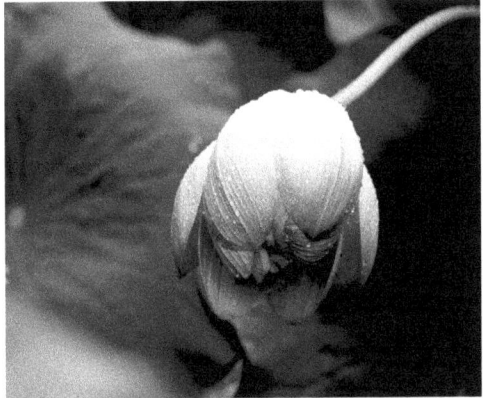

Think of it this way: If you've lived an unhealthy lifestyle with poor diet, no exercise, and self-indulgent habits, when you look in a mirror you may not be pleased with what you see. On the other hand, if you've followed principles of good health expressed through diet, exercise, and self-control, you will see a radiant person reflected back to you.

Neither of these reflections represents who you really are. They simply mirror past choices that you've made. You can change these choices, and their outcome (your karma), as you grow in your understanding of the laws that govern creation.

Here are five ways we can overcome the karma of past wrong actions, given by Paramhansa Yogananda.

### Service to Others

Bad karmic tendencies can be overcome not by concentrating on them, but by developing their opposite good tendencies. This is why service is so important. By serving others, you automatically divert that energy which wants to take you in wrong, self-serving directions.

## Use Your Will Power

"In India there has been too much emphasis on karma. 'Karma! Karma!' they cry. 'It's my karma. I can do nothing about it!' Absurd! Karma is simply action. Whatever has been done can just as certainly be undone."

## Face Your Tests Courageously

In working out karma, as long as you are afraid of it, you won't be completely free. Karma is best worked out by meeting every test that comes, and by courageously accepting any hardship.

## Use Meditation to Work Out Karma

Every time you meditate, your karma decreases, for your energy then is focused in the brain and changes old karmic patterns. After every deep meditation, you will become freer inside.

## The Help of the Guru

"Karma is greatly mitigated by the help of the guru. The guru sees your karma, and knows what you need to do to get out of it. He also assumes much of your karmic burden. . . . Such is the priceless value of the guru's help. Without a guru, the spiritual path is like trying to walk in quicksand when there is a paved highway nearby going in the same direction."

May you walk the highway that leads to freedom from all karma.

*Towards that goal,*
NAYASWAMI DEVI

# NEAR-DEATH EXPERIENCES

I n recent years there have been many books and videos by people who have had near-death experiences. In fact, about one in five people who return from a clinical death (often on an operating table) have had a profound, even life-changing experience.

Paramhansa Yogananda has explained the process of dying: "When the heart begins to grow numb, there is a sense of suffocation because without heart action, the lungs cannot operate. This sense of suffocation is a little painful for only one to three seconds, but because souls reincarnate many times, they retain the memory of this painful feeling of suffocation. This memory causes fear of death.

"During this feeling of suffocation, attachments to possessions and loved ones sometimes come strongly to mind, and there is a struggle to bring the breath back. At this time, a condensed review of all the good and bad actions of this lifetime takes place in the mind of the dying person. The senses of touch, taste, smell, sight, and hearing vanish in succession, with the sense of hearing being the last to leave."

In *Autobiography of a Yogi*, Sri Yukteswar describes the astral world in great detail. But sometimes it is easier to relate to the accounts of "normal people" who have little knowledge of spiritual teachings. I recently learned of such an account: the near-death experience of a young woman who had a dreadful head-on collision and ended up "dying" during an operation. While out of her body she had some deep insights which help us see how entrenched attitudes and habits keep us bound. Here are some important takeaways:

- She heard the silent prayers of her mother, her aunt, and others. Feeling the sorrow in those prayers, she almost wanted to go back. *(Comment: We sometimes question whether prayer is effective, but the souls of those we pray for are helped, sometimes profoundly.)*

- A light beckoned. "The light was so incredible; I had never felt any love like that — a mom's love, romantic love, nothing could compare." In her life review, she felt that God and the angels didn't judge her negatively for the things she had done, although they were sad for some of the choices she had made. They just wanted what was best for her.

- The past as well as the future flashed before her. It wasn't the major events or relationships in her life that were emphasized, but rather her interactions with people who had played small roles. She felt what it was like to be on the receiving end of her actions, and learned the impact she had had on others.

- She saw that the main choice she should have made was to be good to herself, to treasure herself, to treat herself with compassion. Though it was hard for her seeing the mistakes she'd made in life, the overall experience was immensely joyful.

It is enlightening to see that the little choices we make in life can have profound effects on our life's journey. But great lessons come from simple truths: As this woman says, "Love is all that matters; it is all that we take with us when we go."

Swami Kriyananda taught us another simple truth: "Be kind to each other along the way." Life can be joyful or sad depending on whether we make our small, everyday acts ones of love and kindness. The tapestry of our life will be woven from a thousand little threads. It is good to remember Paramhansa Yogananda's advice: "The minutes are more important than the years."

*With love,*

NAYASWAMI JYOTISH

P.S. If you would like to learn more about Tricia Barker's near-death experience, here is her thirty-five-minute account of it: **crystalclarity.com/163**.

# THE SAINT AND THE SCORPION

There is a story about a saint who was peacefully meditating under a tree along the banks of the Ganges. At a certain point he heard a rustling overhead and opened his eyes to see a large scorpion moving along a branch overhanging the river.

When the creature reached the end of the branch, it fell into the water below. Filled with compassion, the saint waded into the river to rescue it. Cupping his hands together, he lifted the drowning scorpion and placed him gently on the river's bank. In return for his kindness, the scorpion stung him.

Unperturbed, the saint then returned to the peace of his meditation. Again he heard a rustling overhead, again the scorpion plunged into the water, and again the saint rescued him, only to be stung.

When this happened a third time, a passerby who had been observing the drama could no longer contain himself. Approaching the saint, he asked, "Sir, why do you continue to rescue the scorpion, when each time he stings you?"

"Well," the saint replied, his eyes luminous with divine love, "you see, it is the nature of the scorpion to sting. He cannot help himself."

"That may be so, reverend sir, but knowing this, why do you continue to rescue him?" the passerby asked.

"You see, my child, I too cannot help myself. It is my nature to help him."

This story provides us with a valuable lesson in how to live. Each of us encounters "human scorpions" filled with venom and spite whose sting can cause us suffering. But whether insect or human being, such creatures are driven by instinct or the compulsions of past karma, and have no choice but to sting whenever they feel threatened.

The saint, by choosing to attune his consciousness to God's love, had the freedom to express that love under all circumstances. Like the saint, we, too, can choose to align our actions with divine love and peace, no matter what is happening around us.

At first this choice requires an act of will, as the ego tries to protect itself. With repeated effort and determination, however, the choice becomes "second nature." Unlike the scorpion driven by instinct, we find that the higher path, illumined by a constant flow of divine grace, opens clearly before us.

In a sense, all decisions in life then become very simple. As a great saint once said, "We have but one decision to make in life: whether to think of God or not." All the rest are details.

Currently we are enjoying the inspiration of our annual Spiritual Renewal Week at Ananda Village. Friends from all over the world have joined us in a wonderful celebration of Master's blessings and teachings. The

*"Full Fall," by Nayaswami Jyotish. Uniting our efforts, we can create a great realm of light that can guide the world forward into a new era of peace and harmony.*

theme for the week is "Uplift Yourself — Uplift the World," exploring how raising our own consciousness improves not only ourselves but the world around us as well.

Just like the saint, we can choose to express divine love and forgiveness no matter how the world behaves. Then we build an inner fortress of higher consciousness which is impenetrable to the forces of darkness. Uniting our efforts, we can create a great realm of light that can guide the world forward into a new era of peace and harmony.

*With joy and blessings in God and Guru,*
NAYASWAMI DEVI

# WHERE THE ANSWERS LIVE

Have you ever lost something and searched for it everywhere? Of course you have! So have we all. You may hunt here and there, but finally a moment comes when you realize, "I've been looking in the wrong place." Unfortunately, we look in the wrong place not only for things but, more importantly, for the answers to our deepest questions.

The answers to important questions lie more in the heart than in the head. Swami Kriyananda told us that true wisdom comes from a combination of pure feeling and discrimination. God has given us both discrimination (buddhi) and feeling (chitta) to navigate this world. But in this age, our purified feeling nature "burns low, and is ill attended." In such an imbalanced age we can rarely see clearly until we are uplifted by the warm currents of the heart.

It is from the heart that intuitive answers whisper to us. After his first great experience of cosmic consciousness, Paramhansa Yogananda said, "I cognized the center of the empyrean as a point of intuitive perception in my heart."

Intuitive answers can only come once we are calm. Recently an elderly friend of ours had lost a container of protein powder. Not only she, but many of her friends searched high and low with no success. Finally, she said, "Let's ask Master for the answer." After they had centered themselves for a few minutes she declared, "Look on the shelf in my bedroom closet."

"We've already looked there," they protested.

"Let's look again," she said, undeterred. Sure enough, there it was. It had fallen over behind some clothing.

Finding something like protein powder is a relatively trivial thing, but the intuitive heart also holds the solutions to more vital questions.

### Your heart knows your true purpose.

Your intuition already knows your unique pathway to spiritual freedom. If you can calm the restless thoughts and listen sensitively to the deep feelings in your heart you will know your purpose in life. Once you have clarity on this, all else will begin to fall into place as you set out on a journey of wonder and discovery.

Ananda Village just celebrated its fifty-third anniversary on July 4th, a date we share with the founding of America. In the beginning, only Swamiji discerned the true purpose of Ananda: not political, but spiritual freedom. He said, "Since we are all seeking the same goal, it will be easier if we gather together and support one another in our quest." He then set about gathering a small group of those attuned to Yogananda's ray and willing to work together. Since our founding a half-century ago, that little group has grown into a worldwide army of truth seekers.

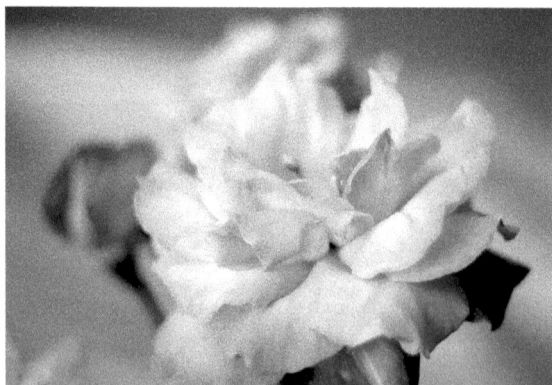

*Your heart knows how to connect to others.*

**Your heart knows how to connect to others.**

In a world filled with polarity and conflict, we need to prioritize loving connections with one another. Divine Mother loves everyone, and if we attune to Her vibration we, too, will feel that everyone is our brother or sister. As long as humanity stays divided, it will continue to find reasons to judge and to hate one another. The desperate need of our time is to give ascendance to acceptance and friendship.

When you are with others, listen and speak to them from your heart. Feel behind their words to their unspoken yearnings and needs. And let both your eyes and words radiate loving balms of kindness and support.

**The heart will lead us to God.**

Most importantly, it is the heart that will lead us to God. In meditation we must go beyond thoughts to find God. As Master's chant says: "Thee I find behind the fringe of my mind."

After the techniques of meditation, sit quietly and *feel* deep devotion in your heart. Go beyond mere thoughts into the deep yearnings of your soul. When the magnet of your love is strong enough, God will no longer be able to stay hidden.

*From the heart,*
NAYASWAMI JYOTISH

# A SHORT MEMORY

"Are you there, God? Are you listening to my prayers? Do you even know what I'm going through?"

I think we all have thoughts like these from time to time — especially when we're facing challenges in life. To keep our faith strong, it's important to remember those times — and we've all had them — when our prayers have in fact been answered.

Recently a friend told me about a trip she'd taken in which she encountered one hurdle after another. The final blow came when she was driving home alone at night from the airport and realized she had a flat tire. Not knowing what to do, she was about to panic when a friend "coincidentally" drove by. He stopped his car and helped her change the tire; soon she was on her way home.

Her story reminded me of an incident in my own life that happened about fifteen years ago — one that I'd forgotten. A friend of mine had been diagnosed with widespread cancer. To slow the disease's advance, she began receiving intravenous chemotherapy. A group of her friends would take turns driving her to the chemo sessions, and would sit with her throughout the day until she was done.

Marilyn (this was her name) was a quiet, gentle soul who was a devoted follower of Yoganandaji. She never complained about her diagnosis, the treatments, the changes they wrought on her body, nor the upheaval the disease caused in her life. She passed away peacefully about a year after this story took place.

On that particular day, Marilyn had finished her latest chemotherapy session, and I was driving her back to Ananda Village.

It was late afternoon; exhausted from the treatment, Marilyn reclined in the passenger seat and drifted off to sleep.

We were a few miles away from Ananda on a rural road, when suddenly I heard the dreaded "thump, thump, thump," and knew we had a flat tire. I pulled over to the side of the road, and not knowing how to change a tire nor seeing anyone around, inwardly I offered a desperate prayer for help.

Just at that moment, an old, beat-up pickup truck pulled over in front of us. Two disreputable-looking characters with long, greasy hair and dirty clothes came over to the car. Since I didn't know what to expect, I cautiously rolled my window down a crack. To my great relief one of them said, "Looks like you ladies can use a little help."

In short order, they changed the tire and were on their way. I was sitting in stunned silence, when Marilyn opened her eyes and quietly asked, "What happened?"

"I think God just heard my prayer," was my quiet reply.

One of the most beautiful and powerful chapters in *Autobiography of a Yogi* is "Two Penniless Boys in Brindaban," in which Yoganandaji's eldest brother, Ananta, challenges him to put his faith in God to a test. Ananta proposes that young Yoganandaji travel to the nearby city of Agra with a friend, Jitendra, but with no money and no return ticket.

To complete the test, they must not beg, reveal their predicament to anyone, nor miss any meals. Further, the boys must see the sights of Agra and return home by train before midnight.

Perhaps feeling some remorse for sending two young boys on such a journey, the skeptical Ananta added: "If by any chance or grace you pass successfully through the Brindaban ordeal, I shall ask you to initiate me as your disciple."

Maybe you are familiar with the rest of the story. While still on the train to Brindaban, they were approached by two strangers who invited them to lunch at their ashram. The meal turned out to be a sumptuous repast prepared for two princes, patrons of the ashram who at the last minute were unable to attend.

(Left to right) Jitendra Mazumdar, companion on the "penniless test" at Brindaban; Lalita-da, Master's cousin; Swami Kebalananda, Master's saintly Sanskrit tutor; and Master, as a high school youth.

As they were leaving the ashram, replete from their elaborate banquet, Jitendra complained, "A fine mess you have got me into! Our luncheon was only accidental good fortune! How can we see the sights of this city, without a single pice between us? And how on earth are you going to take me back to Ananta's?"

Yogananda's reply was one we all need to remember: "You forget God quickly, now that your stomach is filled." His account continues, "My words, not bitter, were accusatory. How short is human memory for divine favors! No man lives who has not seen certain of his prayers granted." (If you haven't read the *Autobiography*, I'll let you discover for yourself how the story ends.)

Indeed, how short our memory is for the graces we have received. As you finish reading these words, I suggest that you take a moment to recall an instance in your own life of an answered prayer, or a feeling of certainty of God's love for you.

The great saints tell us that God's blessings, guidance, and protection are always with us. It is we who too often forget them.

Seeking always to remember,
NAYASWAMI DEVI

# THREE WORDS CAN CHANGE YOUR LIFE

Two travelling monks came upon a stream swollen and roiling due to the recent rains. A woman in distress asked if they could help her. "I must get across the stream to my family," she said, "but I'm afraid to wade into such turbulent water."

One of the monks picked her up, carried her safely across to the other side, and set her down. The two companions then continued on their journey. After several miles the second monk said, "I can't believe you did that, knowing as you do that it is against the rules of our order to look at a woman, much less touch her."

The first monk smiled and replied, "Brother, brother, I set her down on the other side of the stream an hour ago, but you've been carrying her for all these miles."

Many of us suffer from the second monk syndrome — we carry a negative mental dialogue about something we should have set down long ago. It might be the memory of some long-ago hurt or a time we felt betrayed. Or it might be something more recent, an argument or a nagging worry. Whatever the root cause of the negative mental loop, it creates unhappiness.

But how can we set it down? Here is a short phrase, a kind of modern mantra, that will help:

Let it Go.

"We Are One," by Nayaswami Jyotish.

Every time you discover your mind caught in the negative loop, mentally repeat, "Let it Go, Let it Go." After a time—two weeks according to neuroscientists—you will have created a new neural pathway. Now, when something triggers your negative pattern, you can choose to Let it Go.

Paramhansa Yogananda called these neural pathways "brain grooves." He explained, "Attention is the needle that forms the grooves of mental good or bad habits. It is by deep attention to an evil experience or a good experience that a bad or good habit is formed in the brain." At another time he said, "Bad karmic tendencies cannot be overcome by concentrating on them, but by developing their opposite good tendencies."

This technique, of replacing the negative thoughts with positive ones, works in nearly all circumstances of daily life. For devotees, however, its real power comes in meditation. If you find restless thoughts or worries disrupting your concentration, immediately repeat your modern mantra, "Let it Go." Do it with power: The deeper your intention, the quicker you will see results.

Stopping negative patterns is only half the battle—we need also to create a positive flow. For this, a second phrase is helpful. I suggest "I am Free." We can think of it this way: We can use Let it Go to stop the unwanted train of thought and put our mental gears in neutral. Now we can move forward by repeating, "I am Free." Let this phrase continue until it fills your thoughts and you feel a deep sense non-attachment spreading in your consciousness.

Paramhansa ends his magnificent poem, "*Samadhi*," with these words:

> Myself, in everything, enters the Great Myself.
> Gone forever, fitful, flickering shadows of mortal memory.
> Spotless is my mental sky, below, ahead, and high above.
> Eternity and I, one united ray.
> A tiny bubble of laughter, I
> Am become the Sea of Mirth Itself.

*With a bubble of laughter,*
NAYASWAMI JYOTISH

# WHAT CHANGES?

O ur two large suitcases lay partially full on the floor. For the past two weeks, we'd been slowly filling them with clothes and travel items for our trip to Ananda centers in Italy and India. We'll be gone for three and a half months, so planning what to bring for different climes and times has been a bit challenging.

I could feel that my mind was beginning to churn as I weighed different options for what to bring, and tried to form a mental image of all the places to which we'd be going. Movement, time, space — it began to seem a bit overwhelming to me.

Then I remembered a story about a woman who traveled from England to India to visit a great saint there — Ramana Maharshi. Upon meeting him, she said, "I've come all the way from London to see you."

"You haven't moved at all," was his startling reply. "The world around you has moved, but your own center has never changed."

He was telling her that on the deepest level our consciousness is unmoving and not affected by any outer change. Yoganandaji wrote in *Autobiography of a Yogi* that divine sight is center everywhere, circumference nowhere. Every point of the universe can be perceived as the center. You are the center of the universe, and someday you will be able to experience this.

Swami Kriyananda once said, "You don't really move. Space itself is a delusion. You seem to go from here to your home, to India, to Europe, but the world is really moving around you, as far as the perception of it is concerned. You were never moving, but you put yourself at your periphery, so it seems that you were moving all the time."

*Divine sight is center everywhere, circumference nowhere.*

He went on to say, "The same thing is true for time. You have been living a very long time, and yet you haven't been living in time at all, except as you have persuaded yourself that it is real. It's only an illusion in our consciousness."

As I thought about these vast concepts, my mind began to slow down. I sat to meditate, and realized that soon I would be traveling around the world, but that I would be bringing my Self with me wherever I went.

And I knew from past experience that the days of our journey would pass quickly. In the blink of an eye, the next thing I would experience would be sitting in our little meditation room once again. Time and space — they really don't exist as we usually perceive them. We may be dreaming them, but our souls aren't bound by them.

Yoganandaji wrote: "God made man immortal. The plan was for him to remain on earth as an immortal. He was to behold the drama of change with a changeless, immortal consciousness and, after seeing the dance of change on the stage of changelessness, he was to return to the bosom of eternal blessedness."

Silently I offered a prayer of gratitude for the constant guidance of our great teachers, who illumine our lives with their wisdom.

Now I have to get back to those suitcases. . . .

*With joy,*
NAYASWAMI DEVI

# LET THY WILL BE DONE

A friend of ours told us that she has always believed in and used the power of prayer. Since childhood, however, her prayers have gradually become simpler and more focused. Now she repeats only a single prayer every day and for every situation: "Lord, let Thy will be done." This was also the final prayer of Jesus just before his crucifixion. One might call it the ultimate prayer of all great souls.

This prayer provides several profound benefits. For one thing, it allows one truly to follow Yogananda's advice to "remain even-minded and cheerful in all circumstances." A second, more important benefit is that complete self-offering is the most fertile soil in which deep devotion and faith can grow.

When we are caught in the labyrinth of our ego we see only a very distorted reality, filtered through the lens of our moods, desires, and attachments. The distortions of the mind due to the turbulence of the heart are depicted beautifully in a song, "Both Sides Now," by Joni Mitchell.

> Rows and floes of angel hair
> And ice cream castles in the air
> And feather canyons everywhere
> I've looked at clouds that way
>
> But now they only block the sun
> They rain and snow on everyone
> So many things I would have done
> But clouds got in my way

I've looked at clouds from both sides now
From up and down, and still somehow
It's cloud illusions I recall
I really don't know clouds at all

The song goes on to address the themes of love and life in much the same way, with one's positive and negative moods distorting perception until the inevitable conclusion is: *I really don't know love at all*, and *I really don't know life at all*.

Isn't this everyone's dilemma—clouds get in our way? A blossoming of love, faith, and clarity is the real benefit of the prayer, *Let Thy will be done*.

"Faith," by Nayaswami Jyotish.

Paramhansa Yogananda put it this way: "Faith must be cultivated. It cannot be achieved by mere wishful thinking. If you throw yourself off a mountaintop with the affirmation, 'God will protect me,' just see if He does! He expects you to use the common sense He has given you.

"He *will* take care of you, surely, if you do your best always, act sensibly, and leave the results in His hands. Faith, however, must be watered by inner experience, like a plant. The more you actually experience the care He takes of you, the more you will come to rely on Him — not fanatically, but naturally, in the divine way."

He also said, "God doesn't always answer your prayers in the way that you expect, but, if your faith in Him never wavers, He will grant you far *more* than you expect."

Devi and I embark today on our long journey to Italy and India. There are countless unknowns ahead of us, as there are for everyone, every day. Ultimately, anxiety about the future simply takes away our joy. It make a lot more sense to just relax and say lovingly to Divine Mother, "Let Thy will be done."

*In the loving arms of God,*
NAYASWAMI JYOTISH

# IF YOU CAN SEE IT, YOU CAN DO IT

T he throngs of excited travelers moved quickly past us as they dragged their luggage and children along in search of their departure gates. We were in the Frankfurt airport with a long layover waiting for our connecting flight to Rome, and then on to Assisi. We would be spending the next month in Assisi, sharing with our Ananda spiritual family as well as with devotees from all over Europe.

While we waited for our flight, we were frantically studying Italian so that we might have some semblance of facility to converse with our friends. Intently focused as we were, we were surprised when a man suddenly stood before us. He impressed us with the clear, strong energy which shone in his eyes and in the radiance of his smile.

"I've been watching you from across the room," he said, "and when I saw your beautiful smiles, I just had to come over to talk with you."

He began asking us about our lives, and strangely it felt like we were old friends, picking up where we had left off at some other time. He was sincerely interested when we told him about Ananda, the path that we follow, and how we came to dedicate our lives to a spiritual search.

Pierre (our new/old friend) was an American, but he'd been living abroad for the past fifteen years serving as head basketball coach at the Tony Parker Academy, one of the finest athletic academies in Lyon, France. "We coach people from all walks of life—from undefeated pro teams, to high school kids looking for a career in basketball, to people who simply need help and encouragement," he told us.

He listened thoughtfully as we explained how we teach meditation to help people find their own highest potential. Then he looked at us intently, and said, "That's what I do, too, but in a different way. I'll tell you a story about how I work with people."

And this is the story he shared. Pierre had been working with a group of autistic children, using basketball to help them develop self-confidence. The children loved coming to his class, where they were learning how to overcome fears and limitations. All of them had improved in their skills except for one little girl, who remained withdrawn and unable to shoot a basket.

In the gymnasium where they practiced, the front row was an impressive stretch of plush, red-velvet seats which were reserved for VIPs. Pierre had been told by his boss not to let the children use these seats, so as to keep them pristine for the "very important people."

But seeing how hard the kids had worked and how much they had achieved, he said to them at their last class, "If you can make a basket, then you can sit in one of those red-velvet seats."

No sooner had he said this than he realized he had made a terrible mistake. The withdrawn girl would not be able to make a basket, and she would feel even more alienated from the others. One by one each child went to the free-throw line, and one by one they each made a basket. Bursting with happiness, they took a seat in one of the fancy chairs.

Finally it was the turn of the special child. She tried several times and failed. Then Pierre took the ball from her, and said, "Now close your eyes, and see yourself making a basket." After a short time, he asked her, "Did you make it?" "No," was her reply.

"Try again," he encouraged her. "Did you make it now?" Still "no." After repeating this several more times, she finally was able to say with amazement, "I made it!"

Only then did Pierre hand her the ball, and for the first time in her young life, the girl made a basket. The whole class cheered jubilantly for her, and she took her place in one of the special seats — truly a VIP.

After sharing this story, Pierre looked at us deeply and said, "Tell the people that you teach that if they can see it, they can do it."

So, my friends, we share Pierre's love and wisdom with you. No matter how impossible the search for God may seem at times, if you see your soul embraced in His light with enough concentration and aspiration, you will be able to achieve that which you most ardently seek.

*With joy and love from Assisi,*
NAYASWAMI DEVI

# GUIDING PRINCIPLES

S wami Kriyananda gave us two principles which, like moral compass points, guide the guide the Ananda communities. The first is something he saw when visiting the Maharaja of Cooch Behar. The family motto read: *Yato dharma, tato jaya.* This sloka from the great epic, the *Mahabharata*, means, "Where there is adherence to righteousness, there is victory." This ancient "compass point" is the polestar that has allowed India to navigate the turbulent tides of time. If we hold fast to this principle, it will align our actions with the subtle laws of the universe.

Swami Kriyananda's second principle guides our actions in this world: "People are more important than things." This helps us get our priorities right, and is especially important for managing groups of people, such as businesses and communities.

We are currently at the Ananda community near Assisi, Italy, giving classes and satsangs, and meeting with friends. It's been over three years since we last visited, and the changes here are quite amazing. The community and teaching center are extraordinarily vibrant, with people coming from all over Europe, and many moving here. Perhaps Europe is a little ahead of the curve, seeing more clearly the results of all the disruptions — from both pandemic and warfare — that are happening.

We tend to do everything we can to avoid having our lives shaken up, but Divine Mother knows what She is doing. Swami Kriyananda saw that as long as the world was stable, it would trudge along in its familiar ruts, complacent and resistant to change. Divine Mother is making the world less safe, shaking us out of our grooves and forcing us to take a deeper look at our priorities.

A couple of days after we arrived, we met with a small group of future leaders. The difficulties of the last few years were a main topic of conversation. Because the leaders here responded to this crisis by strictly adhering to Ananda's twin principles, everything is flourishing now. Politicians have fanned the flames of separation with fear and anger, but at Ananda, holding fast to dharma and kindness has allowed the troubled waters to bring people together with great purpose, cooperation, and kindness. One person at the satsang used a phrase that I had never heard but will never forget. She called the virus "Saint Covid," because of all the beneficial changes and spiritual growth that it's produced.

*"Babaji and Christ," by Nayaswami Jyotish.*

There is a palpable sense of grace here at Ananda Europa. As *Autobiography of a Yogi* tells us, Jesus appeared to the great master, Babaji, in the Himalayas and asked him to send someone to bring the high teachings of the East, especially meditation, to the West. Paramhansa Yogananda was that chosen ambassador. He, in turn, ignited the heart of Swami Kriyananda, and the result is the worldwide work of Ananda.

As I walked these hills, I had a deep sense that a circle had been completed. The steps go like this: 1) Jesus asks Babaji to send these ancient teachings to the West. 2) Yogananda fulfills that wish. 3) He blesses Swami Kriyananda as his disciple. 4) Swamiji founds an Ananda community here in Assisi, which is widely considered to be the very heart of Christendom. 5) Now at the Ananda community, Babaji and Jesus sit side by side on the high altar.

What a lovely sense of completion. The Masters work in very long rhythms to bring about the spiritual evolution of the planet. The current situation is not the disaster that it may appear on the surface to be. It is, rather, one of the steps needed for our awakening.

Let our hearts be grateful for everything that comes to us.

*In gratitude,*
NAYASWAMI JYOTISH

# IF YOU ONLY KNEW . . .

**CC** **I** f you only knew how much God loved you, you would die for joy." These words from St. Jean Vianney, a French saint of the nineteenth century, have always inspired and motivated me spiritually.

Jyotish and I are visiting Ananda's community and retreat center outside of Assisi now, and are staying in the lovely guest apartment of two good friends, Shantidev and Radhika. On the wall in one of the rooms is a print of a beautiful Indian painting called, "Enter the Spiritual World." It depicts Krishna tenderly embracing one of his devotees in a pastoral setting.

I asked Shantidev what the story was behind the painting, and here is what he recounted. The devotee being embraced is Gopal Kumar, who, in a past incarnation, had been one of the gopis with Krishna in Brindaban. Through subsequent lives of spiritual seeking, Gopal Kumar had become a great yogi.

*"Enter the Spiritual World"*
*(painting from India).*

Now he had reached the stage where all he wanted was to achieve union with God. In his quest he traveled throughout the three worlds — causal, astral, and physical — to find what he was seeking. Still, his life's burning goal eluded him.

Finally he arrived in Goloka Brindaban, the dimension where Krishna resides in the spiritual realm. Here, after many incarnations of separation, he beheld Krishna once again. There was an immediate mutual recognition; Krishna enfolded his dear devotee, Gopal Kumar, in a loving embrace. And just then, to everyone's alarm, Krishna fainted.

All the devotees gasped, not knowing what had befallen their beloved Lord. They fanned him and rubbed his feet, and eventually Krishna returned to consciousness. He explained that he had been so full of ecstasy and joy to meet Gopal Kumar again after their long separation that he had lost consciousness.

What a beautiful thought to reflect upon: *that God is even more ecstatic than we are when one of His lost children returns home*. Jean Vianney described the transcendent joy that comes to that devotee who knows God's love, and Krishna shows us the completion of divine union: God's joy is even greater than our own.

Sometimes it is life's tests and challenges that help us to feel God's love more deeply. Recently while in Assisi, Jyotish and I contracted Covid, which fortunately was a very mild case. Now we are almost totally recovered.

During our illness, we received such an outpouring of love, support, and prayers from friends around the world that we were deeply touched. As we read the many notes, we were moved at how God's love for us is sometimes expressed outwardly through divine friendship. Often when we need it the most, we get glimpses of how much we are loved.

Like Gopal Kumar, let's continue on our journey to find Oneness with God. One day, we will know the fullness of His love and merge with it into ecstasy.

*Your friend in God,*
NAYASWAMI DEVI

# LET GOD DECIDE

evi and I have been spending a month at the Ananda community near Assisi, Italy, where there is great reverence for St. Francis. Paramhansa Yogananda, too, honored him, calling him his "patron saint."

A few years after Ananda's arrival in Italy, word began to reach Swami Kriyananda, who was residing here at the time, that the Bishop of Assisi had been issuing warnings against us. Apparently, Church authorities had come to consider our presence there a threat.

Swami Kriyananda, being a very forthright person, decided to have a talk with him. In many ways they turned out to be kindred souls: both of them highly intelligent, well educated, and sincere in their spirituality. After spending some time discussing spiritual matters, Swamiji was about to take his leave. As he was at the door the Bishop said, "I enjoyed our time together and really like you. Too bad you aren't a Christian."

Swamiji, knowing that it would be useless to argue, replied with a twinkle in his eye, "You say I am not a Christian, and I say I am. Let's let Jesus decide."

This thought, "Let's let God decide," should be like a mantra, a compass that guides our life. It is a shorthand way of saying, "Not my will, nor your will, but God's will." For devotees of this path, we might translate it as, "What would Master do?" or, "What does my own higher Self advise for me?" How many arguments could be avoided if we let this attitude guide us.

Paramhansa Yogananda put it this way: "Learning to love our relatives is simply a training in stretching our consciousness. It is a preliminary practice in loving all others as we do our relations, whom we think of as our own. We have to learn to look on family and strangers alike, because all are children of God. He has given you certain family members with whom you are practicing stretching your consciousness. When the husband serves the wife, and she serves him, each with the desire to see the other happy, Christ Consciousness — God's loving Cosmic Intelligence that permeates every atom of creation — has begun to express itself through their consciousness. Whenever you do something for someone else, without any selfish motive, you have stepped into the sphere of Christ Consciousness."

When we align our heart and mind with those of the stretched consciousness of a master, we have a polestar to guide us. If we could simply remember to ask the question, "What do you advise?" most problems in life, and especially in relationships, could be avoided.

Devi and I have recently finished a ten-class course, *How to Develop Harmonious Relationships*. In it we explore all facets of relationships of every kind: personal and intimate ones as well as others such as friendships and those that are work-related.

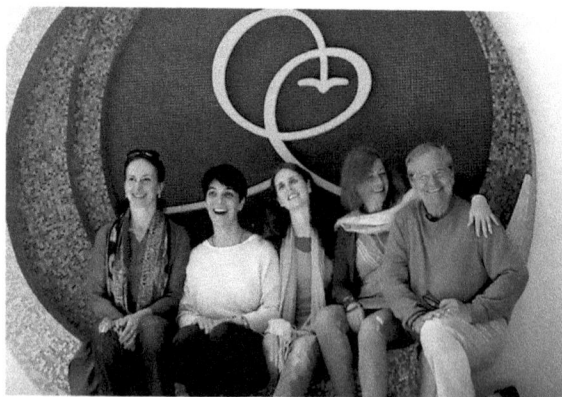

*Devotees at the Ananda Assisi community in Italy.*

Ultimately, all relationships are expressions of the Christ consciousness, but the more we are caught up in desires, attachments, and ego, the more conflicts arise. Human emotions, especially negative ones, are a labyrinth with no exit. The only real solution is to rise above the limiting walls of ego into the free skies of higher consciousness. How? By remembering to ask God or a master, "What do you advise here?"

Asking is one part of the picture. Listening for His response is the other part. God won't intrude on our free will, so we must first be truly ready to accept His advice. Then we must allow our minds and emotions to become still. He loves us as His very own, and is waiting for us to turn to Him. When we do, He will answer us with a soft and loving whisper.

The next time you are about to argue a point, follow Swami Kriyananda's model and say, perhaps with a twinkle in your eye, "Let's let God decide."

In His all-embracing love,
NAYASWAMI JYOTISH

# 36

*September 9, 2022*

# LET IT SHINE

Today is our last day in the Ananda community near Assisi. In a few days we'll be flying to India to greet friends whom we haven't seen for three years and to experience the expansion of Ananda's work there. Our time in Assisi has been filled with blessings as we've shared together with our gurubhais the joy of a life in God.

It's especially heartening to see the dedicated young people and families who are moving here. There seems to be a new generation of spiritually advanced souls being born who aren't impressed with the razzle-dazzle of the world, but are seeking higher values.

A friend of ours was telling us about a group of children whose families have recently moved to Assisi and who have asked him to teach them meditation. One twelve-year-old girl told him that she'd been reading Swami Kriyananda's *Art and Science of Raja Yoga*, and had written a school paper on Patanjali's *Yoga Sutras*.

"I'm very interested in the *yamas* and *niyamas*," the girl told our friend, "and especially in the principle of non-lying. Before we moved here, when I was with my friends at school, I would pretend to be interested in clothes so that they would accept me. Now I realize after coming to Ananda that I was lying to myself, because that isn't really who I am." What a profound insight, something that most people never realize!

Hearing this story reminded me of an experience I myself had had shortly after coming to Ananda Village in 1969. In the first days after arriving, I felt a great sense of freedom that I didn't quite understand. Then one day the words clarified in my mind: "I don't have to play games anymore."

I understood that I could be myself without trying to impress others according to their standards — ones that I didn't share.

Nayaswami Jyotish and Nayaswami Devi at the Ananda Assisi community temple.

This is a gift of the spiritual path: to discover and accept our own uniqueness, and let it determine the course of our life. As the young girl who was exploring non-lying discovered, self-honesty requires courage, but only then are we able to live our life with authenticity.

We were speaking with another friend at Assisi, and told her about the man at Frankfurt airport that I wrote about in an earlier blog. He had looked very penetratingly at Jyotish and me and said, "You have to accept your own light so that other people have the courage to accept theirs."

After hearing this story, Sahaja got a surprised look in her eyes, and got up and left the room. She soon returned holding a small carved wooden angel that she'd had on her altar for many years. It contained an excerpt from the writings of Marianne Williamson:

Our deepest fear is not that we are inadequate. Our deepest fear is that we are powerful beyond measure. It is our light, not our darkness, that most frightens us. We ask ourselves, "Who am I to be brilliant, gorgeous, talented, fabulous?" Actually, who are you *not* to be? You are a child of God. Your playing small does not serve the world. There is nothing enlightening about shrinking so that other people won't feel insecure around you. We are all meant to shine, as children do. We were born to make manifest the glory of God that is within us. It's not just in some of us; it's in everyone. And as we let our own light shine, we unconsciously give other people permission to do the same. As we are liberated from our own fear, our presence automatically liberates others.

Finally, remember that it isn't for our own aggrandizement that we accept the divine light within us. As Christ told his followers: "Let your light so shine before men, that they may see your good works, and glorify your Father who is in heaven."

When we can stand in humility, bathed in God's light within and without, then we experience the truth of who we really are.

*Wishing you the joy of Self-discovery,*
NAYASWAMI DEVI

# MY BODY TOUCHED THAT SOD

Devi and I are once again in India after an absence of more than three years. There is a palpable sense of the Divine here, which Paramhansa Yogananda highlighted on March 7, 1952, as he uttered the last words of his incarnation. Swami Kriyananda recounted that momentous event in *The New Path*:

> Master was scheduled to speak after the banquet. His brief talk was so sweet, so almost tender, that I think everyone present felt embraced in the gossamer net of his love. Warmly he spoke of India and America, and of their respective contributions to world peace and true human progress. He talked of their future cooperation. Finally he read his beautiful poem, "My India."
>
> Throughout his speech I was busy recording his words, keeping my eyes on my notebook. He came to the last lines of the poem:
>
> > Where Ganges, woods, Himalayan caves, and men dream God.
> > I am hallowed; my body touched that sod!
>
> "Sod" became a long-drawn-out sigh. Suddenly from all sides of the room there came a loud cry.

Though we have been here for only a few days, on some subtle plane I, too, feel hallowed that my feet are touching this sacred land. One can feel an elusive holiness in the very air of this land. Swami Kriyananda writes, "God chooses those who choose Him."

Over and again through the long mists of time, great souls who have inhabited India have chosen God.

Nor is it only the great saints who focus their lives around a relationship with the Divine. The head of our charitable work in Brindaban, which takes care of thousands of widow-mothers, told us this story:

One of the care workers came upon an elderly lady who was quite upset, muttering to herself, "He hasn't eaten for two days, and I'm getting quite hungry. I am going to have to get a stick and beat him until he agrees to eat. I don't know what to do with that naughty Krishna." She had made a vow, you see, to feed her beloved Krishna before she would take food herself.

*Paramhansa Yogananda on the Ganges during his return trip to India in 1935.*

Master starts his great book, *Autobiography of a Yogi*, with these words, "The characteristic features of Indian culture have long been a search for ultimate verities and the concomitant disciple-guru relationship."

As I write this, it is September 12th, the anniversary of Swami Kriyananda meeting Yogananda. Swamiji showed us, in the clearest possible way, how to draw God's grace. As he knelt for the first time at his guru's feet, he uttered those simple, yet life-changing words that draw God's love: "I want to be your disciple."

Those enchanted words are, of course, only the first step: an affirmation that starts the process of transformation. They must then be reinforced by the discipline of discipleship, by a daily practice of meditation, and by deep self-offering. This, too, Swami Kriyananda modeled for us in every imaginable way. His discipleship to Master became the very core of his self-definition.

We can all choose to do the same. That devotee of Krishna offered her love in the form of physical food. But yogis must offer the ego itself to God. Over time, as we do so, the veils of separation become ever more transparent. Then, our lives, too, become hallowed.

In divine friendship,
NAYASWAMI JYOTISH

# A CELEBRATION OF GOD

A small group of us just returned from a glorious trip to Varanasi, Kolkata, and Serampore — all places known for their holiness, and filled with events sacred to our line of gurus. Everywhere we saw and experienced the joyful celebration of God in many things that is characteristic of life in India, a celebration not somber and serious, but filled with exuberance.

The evening we arrived in Varanasi, we visited the ashram of Ananda Moyi Ma, the great woman saint about whom Yoganandaji writes in *Autobiography of a Yogi*. We meditated there on the balcony overlooking the Ganges next to the room where Ma did puja to her beloved image of Krishna, and in her small bedroom. As we sat quietly, a small boy appeared and began doing cartwheels, laughing all the while. How pleased Ma must have been, I thought, to have so much joy expressed before her.

Early the next morning we visited the home of Lahiri Mahasaya, where he lived, initiated people into Kriya, and left his body. Though the building is locked, there is a large stone bench across the narrow lane on which we sat to meditate. Despite the steady stream of people walking to work, children on their way to school, and noisy motorcycles, we felt a deep inner stillness.

At a certain point, I opened my eyes to see that many of those passing by stopped at Lahiri's door and touched it to take his blessings. A motorcycle driven by a father with his three children on their way to school also stopped, and each one took blessings. What a wonderful way to start the school day!

Our time in Kolkata was one long celebration with Yoganandaji and his disciples. Our wonderful center leaders there, Dithi and Alok, along with a team of devotees, have renovated the house of Master's boyhood friend, Tulsi Bose. It's quite near to Master's family home, and it is at the Bose house that Guruji spent most of his days as a teenager.

Made holy by visits from great saints like Sri Yukteswar, Ananda Moyi Ma, and Vivekananda, and by the many holy relics from Babaji and our line of gurus, the house is beautifully kept now, with all the relics carefully placed in glass cases. Here we all chanted and meditated with the Kolkata devotees, and felt awash with joy.

*The Ghosh family home at 4 Gurpar Road.*

Next we stopped at the Ghosh family home at 4 Gurpar Road, and were lovingly hosted by Master's great-nephew, Somnath, and his wife Sarita. After meditating in the little attic room where Yoganandaji tells us he "first found God," we were served a delicious homemade lunch. One of our group said, "It felt like a family reunion."

After a few more days of public events in Kolkata, we took a beautiful boat ride on the Ganges at twilight to Serampore. It is here, on the riverbank, that the banyan tree still stands where Babaji appeared to Sri Yukteswar and where Sri Yukteswar's ashram is located. As we walked to our hotel, we stopped to pray at the holy tree.

At this time of year, it is customary to celebrate Durga Puja, a ten-day holiday in honor of Durga, the goddess of strength, determination, victory, and wisdom. As part of the festival, large images of Durga are fashioned out of clay, beautifully painted and decorated, and then immersed in the Ganges to let her dissolve back into the Infinite.

As we prayed at the banyan tree, many groups of people carrying their images of Durga released her into the river lovingly, laughingly, joyfully. What a beautiful moment it was!

So many blessings have come thus far on our trip, but the main insight I want to share with you is this: The path to God can be a celebration, a joyful release of all that we are into the infinite arms of God. Yes, we need determination to continue, but don't forget to celebrate God's presence every step of the way. This is what draws us closer to Him.

*With joy and blessings to you,*
NAYASWAMI DEVI

# SIMPLE STEPS TO HAPPINESS

Paramhansa Yogananda said that everyone in the world is motivated by the same twin desires: "to be happy and avoid pain." Each of us can take some simple, and yet surprisingly effective strides toward that goal. Even a series of little steps can produce great changes if we apply them consistently.

The road to happiness starts by replacing bad habits with good ones. Many people have a tendency to focus primarily on physical habits such as diet and exercise. But since we have a body, mind, and soul, we need to address all three aspects.

Swami Kriyananda wrote, "During an interview with newspapermen Master prescribed the following rules as a good daily regimen for all: 'Morning and evening sit in introspective silence thinking of your most important engagement with the soul within. Exercise fifteen minutes. Walk thirty minutes. Study one hour. Meditate one hour and a half. Smile from within all hours.'"

A recent study at the University of California at Berkeley revealed some very helpful and hopeful information. Working with more than 70,000 people involved with an initiative called "The Big Joy Project," scientists found that you can quickly gain a 25% boost in your happiness level by consciously doing "micro-acts of joy." The study shows that these "micro-acts" led to increased feelings of hope, optimism, and happiness.

It works this way: Every day for seven consecutive days, do a small act to boost your emotional well-being. For example, make a gratitude list or keep a gratitude journal. Another practice would be to visit a sick friend or do a nice gesture for someone you know, or even better, for a stranger. Yet another micro-act would be to reframe something you think of as negative into a positive perspective.

Much of the benefit of this practice comes from the conscious decision to make a plan for the week, and then to carry out your daily act of "micro-joy." What better time to start this than the day after Thanksgiving? Take a few moments right now to think about those things for which you are grateful. Write a few notes of gratitude to those who have helped or uplifted you during the year.

Now make a plan for next week of seven daily acts of micro-joy. Doing this will help us reprogram our mental habits. Paramhansa Yogananda said, "Don't expect to go to heaven unless you carry a portable heaven within your heart every day." He also gave this counsel: "If you find your thoughts carried away, little by little, as prisoners of temptation, then you should train your armies of self-control. Seek good company, take right care of the body, and keep your thoughts busy with wonder and bliss of God."

Finally, and most important, is a daily practice of deep meditation. Sometimes meditators can become discouraged by a lack of experiences. But Master said, "Do not grieve because you do not see light or images in meditation. If you go deep into the perception of bliss you will find there the actual presence of God. Seek the Whole, not a part."

If we do our part and make an effort, God will reach out to help us. One time Master blessed a disciple who was having a hard time financially. The anxiety-ridden student asked Master how he could stay so calm in the face of troubles. The Master looked at him intently and said, "Remember, the same Father who protects me, protects you. He is our common Father."

Replacing bad habits with good ones is important, but the greatest thing we can do to improve happiness is to bring God into every aspect of life, and offer everything we have and are into His light. Faith and gratitude are the cures for all our ills.

*In joyful gratitude,*
NAYASWAMI JYOTISH

# PINK MAN

My major field of study in college was cultural anthropology. One of my professors shared some interesting experiences he'd had during a year in which he lived with a remote tribe in New Guinea. These people were so inaccessible that they'd never seen a Westerner before.

At first they just ignored him or stared at him suspiciously as though he were a new variety of albino snake or toad. After weeks of such treatment, he would withdraw into his tent, read Shakespeare, and try to affirm, "I am an educated, intelligent human being who is part of an advanced civilization."

Little by little the tribe's people saw that he meant them no harm, and they allowed him to enter into their daily life. As he began to learn their language and culture, he realized that what they'd been calling him all along was "Pink Man."

After more time had passed, he no longer had to affirm who he had been, but could accept that he was now a different version of himself. After a year, "Pink Man" returned to his university and wrote an ethnography of the tribe that had opened his eyes to another worldview and helped change how he thought about himself.

Considering the professor's experience, I realized that what interested me was not so much the customs and languages of other peoples, but the opportunity to expand one's self-definition by immersing in a different reality. Fortunately, God showed me a better way to do this through the spiritual path and discipleship.

Inner self-transformation is never easy, no matter how you approach it. In trying to transcend self-limitations and old ways of thinking, we find ourselves clinging to the familiar, even if it no longer serves our aspirations.

In Paramhansa Yogananda's unparalleled explanation of the Bhagavad Gita, he tells us that the challenges Arjuna faces before the battle of Kurukshetra are allegorical. Each character, friend or foe, is symbolic of an inner quality that lives within each of us.

Those on the opposing side, the Kauravas, are his relatives and mentors, although they represent such things as material desire, ego, habits, and attachment. As the great warrior Arjuna surveys the Kaurava army before the battle begins, he becomes discouraged, drops his bow, and says to his charioteer, Krishna, "These are my kinsmen. I cannot kill them. Therefore, I will not fight."

Yoganandaji explains that this is the inner battle we all must face. We fear killing old patterns and habits, because we're not sure who we will become when the familiar is gone. Yet unless we take up the fight, we can never discover our own higher Self.

In the remainder of the Gita, Krishna explains to Arjuna that the true Self is never lost, but through spiritual effort, its energy is transmuted into a higher expression. "The soul is never touched; it is immutable, all-pervading, calm, unshakable; its existence is eternal." (2:24)

As Jyotish and I enter our second month of traveling to Ananda centers in Italy and India, the process of personal transformation and letting go of the familiar is something we face daily. What a joy to offer oneself up to the process, allowing God to guide us toward inner freedom.

Whether through the example of "Pink Man" overcoming the fear of loss of self-identity, or Arjuna transcending the reluctance to fight old mental tendencies, we need to take the leap of faith. It's by surrendering the self to God that we go beyond our limitations and find who and what we really are: a spark of the Divine.

*With joy,*
NAYASWAMI DEVI

# A SACRED GIFT

D evi wrote recently about our pilgrimage to sacred sites in Varanasi, Kolkata, and Serampore. On our last day in Serampore a very special gift was given to us.

This city is on the banks of the Ganges and was the location of Sri Yukteswar's ashram, where Paramhansa Yogananda spent the better part of ten years in training with his beloved guru. During that period, Yogananda often visited the family of his elder brother, Anantalal Ghosh, who also resided in Serampore.

We had lunch with members of the Ghosh family. We have known Durlov and his son Ishan for years, having first met them many years ago with Swami Kriyananda. At the end of the meal we withdrew to a private patio where they presented us with an extremely precious plate that had been in the family for well over one hundred years. Here is a description given to us by Ishan of this sacred relic:

"The object which we gave you is a plate made of stone. My father heard from his grandmother, that is, the wife of Anantalal Ghosh, that this plate was there when she was married. That means it must have been bought by either Guruji's parents or someone else in the family in or before the year Anantalal Ghosh was married. Plates like this are usually used in Indian families for offering food to the gods. Usually, they rest at family altars, and so was the case with this plate as well. However, when Paramhansa Yogananda became a sanyasi, it was not possible for him to accept food at home, since all of the kitchen plates were somehow in touch with meat or fish. Therefore, he was offered food instead on plates from the altar; the plates in which food has been offered to the gods; the plate which we gave you. When Paramhansa Yogananda came back to India, he had his meals on these plates as always. This plate has been there in our family for more than a hundred years, and we gifted it to you since we feel that more people should have the opportunity to drink from its spiritual vibrations. We are so pleased that the gods gave us the opportunity to forward such priceless spiritual vibrations into your hands. We are so pleased that you accepted it with such deep reverence and joy."

Presently the plate rests on the lap of a statue of Master that sits in our meditation room in Delhi. We will soon place it along with other sacred objects where visitors and pilgrims can meditate and feel the holy vibrations.

The plate also embodies a deep spiritual lesson for us all. Food is a symbol of the gift of life from Divine Mother, and Yogananda would only eat if the food had first been offered back to God. But *everything* is a gift from Divine Mother, and God-offering should be applied to all aspects of life. Yogananda spoke of this truth poetically in his beautiful poem "God! God! God!"

When we first rise from slumber, the day ahead should be offered to God. When we break our fast, we should be aware that the very food we eat is a form of Divine Mother. If, during our working hours, the spotlight of our mind ever keeps returning to God, our work can be transformed into sacred service. Giving God our worries, our memories, and our dreams transforms the mundane into the sacred. Ultimately, it is our love above all that must be purified through offering it to God.

Gradually, all that we "own," and all that we think we "are," must be offered into God's light. He will receive our offerings, purify them, and then playfully join us in a life free from attachment to the delusion of "I" and "mine."

Isn't is interesting that the essence of the spiritual path is somehow magically condensed into a single sacred plate?

*In the light,*
NAYASWAMI JYOTISH

# I SEE NO STRANGER

The beautiful plaque on the wall of our friends' home caught my eye. We were in Chandigarh staying with a Sikh family who are fellow disciples of Paramhansa Yogananda. They welcomed us with such graciousness and warmth that we soon felt totally at home.

The most prominent feature of the plaque that had drawn my attention was a striking drawing of the Golden Temple at Amritsar, the most sacred site for the Sikhs. What stood out the most for me, however, was a small poem at the bottom:

> I see no stranger, I see no enemy; I look upon all with goodwill. . . . The one Beloved dwells in all. Beholding this wonder, I bloom with joy.

These words were written nearly five hundred years ago by Guru Arjan Dev, the fifth guru in the Sikh lineage. It was he who built the holy temple at Amritsar, and who created the first rendition of the Sikh holy book, the *Guru Granth Sahib*, which is housed there. This sacred text is a collection of his own poetry, and that of others in the line of ten Sikh gurus, as well as a number of Hindu and Muslim saints.

Uplifted by the drawing of the magnificent temple and those beautiful words, I was then stunned to read about the conclusion of this great soul's life: In 1606 Guru Arjan was tortured to death by the invading Mughal emperor Jahangir.

"How little the world has changed," I thought. Here we are still today with Hindu against Muslim, Muslim against Christian, Christian against Jew; with racism against Blacks; with one political party against the other; with one nation against another: the list could go on and on.

How can this ever end? It is only by the upliftment of consciousness. In the teachings of India, the term "maya" is used to denote "delusion." To bring everything into manifestation, God divided His infinite consciousness into pairs of opposites, creating light and darkness, good and evil, joy and sorrow, male and female.

The literal meaning of "maya" is the "measurer," that which divides the undifferentiated whole into seemingly different parts. The tension created by these dichotomies keeps us engrossed in the play of life, until our souls tire of the endless cycling between conflicting opposites. Then we crave to realize the underlying unity of all things, in which we see the One Consciousness behind the many forms.

"I Am the Sky," by Nayaswami Jyotish. "Under one sky we live watched by One Father."

I do believe that, contrary to current appearances, the human race is moving toward this higher perspective. Personal and global suffering are helping us to see that when one is oppressed, we all are oppressed; when one loses his security or freedom, we all lose it. This awareness must come in time, because in essence we are not separate one from another. God manifested each of us out of His own consciousness; we are all equally parts of Him.

Some years ago, a friend gave us an original edition of Paramhansa Yogananda's book of poetry, *Songs of the Soul*, which was signed by him personally. His inscription reads: "There is one breath that enlivens all strange lands and strangers. Under one sky we live watched by One Father. With my blessings, Swami Yogananda, Oct. 20, 1924."

May we all awaken to that consciousness in which, blessed by one Father, we see no strangers.

*With hope,*
NAYASWAMI DEVI

# THE RETURN OF THE LIGHT

"They're coming! Our king and queen are coming! Ram, our beloved God, and Sita, our beautiful queen, are finally coming home!" Thus rejoiced the happy citizens of Ayodhya centuries ago when Ram and Sita returned. After long years away, the living light was returning to Ayodhya, and the people were placing lamps along the road to celebrate the occasion.

This event, central to the Ramayana (one of two great spiritual epics of India), has inspired people for thousands of years. Even today the victory of light over darkness fills a deep soul-longing in the heart of humanity.

Diwali, the Festival of Light, is celebrated throughout India. Lights can be seen everywhere: strings of it decorating balconies and windows, candles placed in doorways and windows and on the altars of homes, and fireworks bursting like stars in the night sky. It's not only in India that Diwali is celebrated. In New York City it is an official public holiday, given that there are over 200,000 people of Indian origin living there. Diwali is celebrated in the White House and, of course, in the U.K., which now has the first prime minister of Indian origin. The light of Diwali is, indeed, spreading around the world.

Of course, these outward displays are what might be called "social Diwali." Spiritual Diwali is our daily return to the light in the spiritual eye, which can be experienced in every meditation.

Throughout long cycles of time, this theme — the triumph of light over darkness — has recurred in many different forms. For much of the Western world, it is celebrated at Christmas time, when the Christ was born. Each race and culture recognizes and celebrates light in its own special way.

This holy season is a good time to open our hearts, to recognize and give thanks to the people and events that have been channels for God's light and love to us. For many of our readers, our "Diwali" is the coming of Paramhansa Yogananda, often experienced when we first read *Autobiography of a Yogi*. Take a moment to reflect on how God has come into your life, and offer prayers of gratitude. Meditate for a while on all the people — family, friends, and teachers — who have been channels of Divine Mother's love to you.

*Painting by Nayaswami Jyotish, "The Light of Love."*

One of the things that Devi and I try to do in these weekly essays is to share little moments of inspiration that occur in our lives. As a Diwali gift we were given a small book, *365 Quotes by Gandhi*, and I thought it would be nice to share with you a few rays of Gandhi's light.

"You may never know what results come of your actions, but if you do nothing there will be no results."

"Whenever you are confronted with an opponent, conquer him with love."

"The day the power of love overrules the love of power, the world will know peace."

In a Diwali talk that Swami Kriyananda gave in India in 2004, he urged everyone to fully open themselves to God's light. That, however, is not enough. He went on to say that we should also strive to see the light of God in everyone we meet, and that we must actively spread God's love to a world that desperately needs it.

Let each of us be a channel of light and live every day as if it were Diwali, a new dawning of the divine light.

*In God's light,*
NAYASWAMI JYOTISH

# BRING ME A MUSTARD SEED

The woman sobbed inconsolably as she pressed the body of her dead child to her bosom. A sympathetic neighbor, on seeing her so overwhelmed with grief, said, "A saint has come to visit our village. Perhaps he can perform a miracle and bring your child back to life."

Gathering the body of her child in her arms, the woman rushed to the feet of Buddha, for it was indeed he to whom the neighbor had been referring. "Sir," she sobbed, holding up the lifeless little form, "can you bring my child back to life?"

With a heart filled with compassion and wisdom, Buddha replied, "My daughter, first bring me a mustard seed from a home that has not known death and suffering."

Desperately she went from house to house, but alas at each one she heard a similar story: "We have lost our beloved father." "Our dear son passed away last month." "Since our mother who cared for us died there is no one to look after us." On and on she went throughout the village, even to the huts in the outlying areas, but nowhere could she find anyone who had not known death and loss.

Finally, exhausted, she returned to Buddha with no mustard seed. Touching his feet, she said, "Lord, now I have understood. Death and suffering visit us all." Buddha then blessed her, her grief lifted, and her heart was comforted.

The saints of all religions teach that everything in life is transitory. All human suffering is caused by seeking permanence in an impermanent world. Only through inner detachment can we find lasting peace.

Globally, we now find ourselves in a world filled with suffering, as environmental, social, financial, and political tensions move us toward an uncertain future. How can we find comfort in such times?

Jyotish and I are now in Pune, India, where last weekend the Ananda Center here hosted an inspiring and powerful daylong spiritual fair attended by many hundreds of people. The keynote talk we'd been asked to give was entitled, "Stand Unshaken: How to Face Change with Courage." Here are four points that we shared to help people deal with uncertainty, change, and loss.

First, when difficulties come, don't ask self-pityingly, "Why me?" Ask rather, **"What am I supposed to learn from this?"** All of life's experiences, whether individually or societally, are given to us to expand our awareness. If we can depersonalize our suffering, and try to see the bigger picture, everything becomes a source of greater understanding and growth.

Next, when going through challenges, try to **find ways to be of service to others**. We have a devotee friend in India who lost his teenaged son to leukemia; two weeks later his father passed away from Covid. What was his response to such grief? He called his nearby Ananda Center and asked, "What can I do to help others?" He became a part of our twenty-four-hour hotline to bring comfort to those experiencing grief and fear during the pandemic. Through his service, he found acceptance of his own loss.

Then, of great importance: **practice meditation**. Through this discipline we can develop inner detachment that will enable us to weather any outer storm. Peace of mind, awareness of a reality greater than our own ego, inner strength: all these and more are the fruits of meditation.

Finally, **deepen your devotion and your faith in God**. The plan for this world is rooted in God's love for us all. Whatever challenges come your way, try to remember that God, with infinite love and patience, is bringing every one of us the experiences we need to find soul freedom.

In a letter that Paramhansa Yogananda wrote to one of his disciples, Kamala Silva, he says, "No matter what dark territories you have to pass through, look steadily at the Polestar of his Presence. He knows you are trying to reach Him, only keep trying. Once you convince Him, you will be there. The way is long, let's hurry to His place. With unceasing blessings, Swami Yogananda."

Like the grieving mother, we can find no place in this world that is without sorrow and suffering. And so, "Let us hurry to His place." It is only there that we will find true peace and joy.

In divine friendship,
NAYASWAMI DEVI

# BEHIND THE STERN FAÇADE

We recently heard a remarkable story about Sri Yukteswar. Many devotees have a little difficulty relating to him, since he seems a bit forbidding. Perhaps it is because in *Autobiography of a Yogi*, Paramhansa Yogananda writes about him in his role as both teacher and disciplinarian, a job he took very seriously, especially knowing that he was preparing Master for a world-changing role.

But the grandson of Tulsi Bose, Master's close friend, told us that when Sri Yukteswar visited their home he was completely different. He was a kind, lovable, grandfatherly figure who usually had sweets to offer to the many children who gathered around him. I, myself, had an experience where I felt his sweetness.

We were about to begin a Kriya Initiation in Chennai, India, and the pictures on the altar were all gar- landed. As I was bowing to each of our Masters, I mentally prayed to Sri Yukteswar to help me relate to him more deeply. The instant the prayer formed in my mind, the garland around his photo fell off, and I was given the opportunity to lovingly re-garland him.

Here, then, is the remarkable story related to us by Nayaswami Aditya, our center leader in Pune:

Mr. Bhuvan Pal Singh joined the online classes in Pune during the first wave of Covid and became a Kriyaban. I immediately recognized him as someone who felt like an old friend. He was sincere, with deep yearning and humility, and asked many questions to refine his spiritual practices.

Mr. Bhuvan's lifelong yearning had been to leave everything and go to the Himalayas, but he found himself supporting his entire extended family of thirty-five people, something he did quite happily and very well. During the first wave of the pandemic he took retirement from his successful corporate career.

Soon after Bhuvan began his Kriya practice, he was diagnosed with a rare malignant cancer of the muscles of his right forearm. Expert advice from the best doctors in the country informed him that little could be done.

With tears in his eyes Bhuvan related this story: "One day I was undergoing a PET scan to assess the spread of the tumor in my body and found myself alone in a hospital room. As I sat there I prayed to the Masters, 'I am feeling very alone.' I instantly had a vision of the form of Sri Yukteswarji in front of me. As his life-size form slowly moved towards me, it shrunk in size until he became very small and entered into my body through my spiritual eye. From within I heard Swami Sri Yukteswarji say, 'Bhuvan, don't feel alone or afraid, for I am in every cell of your body.'"

Bhuvanji continued his daily Kriya practice, and although he followed the suggested treatments, his health deteriorated over the months and on 26 January 2022 he left his body.

Two days later, his wife, Anupama, had the following experience:

"I was awakened early one morning by the sound of the main door of our house being unfastened. As I opened my eyes, I saw a bright yellow light falling on the door, and curious to see what this light was, I moved towards it. Just then I heard and saw my husband, in physical form, seated in the living room in meditative pose, his gaze uplifted. He said to me, 'Anupama, don't move. I'm exiting now.'

"I stood still, and watched my husband exit into that light. A couple of hours after this experience I got a call from my niece in New Delhi. She told me that the previous night she had dreamt that she saw a bright yellow light fall on our house, especially on the main door. In the dream she saw her uncle Bhuvan enter that light."

Anupama has kindly given Nayaswami Aditya permission, and we thank her for allowing us to share this sacred experience.

Soon after Swamiji's passing Devi and I had a "Nadi" reading from an ancient book of prophecy. During that reading we were told that Yogananda was watching out for us minute by minute and second by second. This applies to all of us who have opened our hearts to this great line of masters. Yoganandaji, as Swami Kriyananda explained,[*] was a Blissavatar (incarnation of divine joy). Yoganandaji described Sri Yukteswar as a gyanavatar (incarnation of wisdom). In fact, in God's light all His qualities merge into one, and in our hour of need we, too, will find that God's light is in every cell of our body.

In God's light,
NAYASWAMI JYOTISH

---

* In his essay "Bliss-Avatar?" in *Religion in the New Age and Other Essays for the Spiritual Seeker*, available from Crystal Clarity Publishers.

# A GLOBAL CIRCLE OF LOVE

This is a special moment in time for Jyotish and me. Yesterday we had our last public satsang in Mumbai after nearly four months of traveling, teaching, and sharing love with friends in Assisi and India. By the time you read this, we will be returning to Ananda Village.

In many ways, this trip has been life-changing. Seeing the waves of devotion to Yoganandaji spreading throughout the world, we realize how blessed we've been to be a part of this great work started by Swami Kriyananda over fifty years ago.

*Nayaswami Jyotish and Nayaswami Devi with the Ananda Assisi community.*

Thousands of new students are studying Master's teachings in person and online, and thousands more are taking discipleship and initiation into Kriya Yoga. What touched us the most, however, was seeing the divine love for others that is being offered by Ananda devotees throughout the world. Here are three stories that we heard during our travels.

The first was told to us by Mahiya, one of the leaders of Ananda Assisi. It took place at Terre di Luce (Lands of Light), their beautiful organic gardens:

This summer, Satya, a Kriyaban friend, came to help us in the kitchen. He brought his parents with him: Adamo, ninety-two years old, and Eleonora, in her eighties.

While Satya did his service in the kitchen, they would sit on the sofas and just be. Often people would sit with them, making conversation and expressing kindness. Satya had told them nothing about this path, and they had no idea what Ananda was.

Eleonora has dementia, but Adamo was fully aware of everything. He loved it here, and wanted to participate in everything! When Satya tried to leave them at the nearby house he had rented, Adamo would have nothing of it — he wanted to be at Terre di Luce!

Every afternoon after lunch we have a chanting circle before we start our service. We would often chant to the Guru or to Divine Mother in Sanskrit. The fact that it was all in a strange language didn't matter to Adamo — he would never miss the chanting circle! After one circle he said, "This place is a paradise. I want to stay here forever. Here you are all friends, and everybody loves and respects one another. You can't find that in the world."

Two weeks after Satya and his parents went back to Rome, Adamo left his body. We had an Astral Ascension Ceremony for him in which everyone shared deeply how much this wonderful soul loved Ananda. We all felt that his wish of "wanting to stay at Ananda forever," or in the presence of the Masters that he felt here, had come true: He was now in the astral world in the loving hands of our Masters.

This is what Terre di Luce is for me and why I love it here. I see it as a place where people come and experience love and friendship which transforms them.

The stories of kindness and compassion from our travels in India are too numerous to tell (I'll share a few more in the recorded commentary), but two others especially stand out. India was hit very hard by the pandemic, with many deaths and inadequate supplies of medicine, oxygen, and hospital beds. Our center leaders told us that they were often performing eight to ten Astral Ascension Ceremonies per week for members or their loved ones who had passed.

Two dear Kriyaban friends of ours, Dr. Mansi and Dr. Amar, shared stories about serving together on the Covid ward in a hospital in Pune. They're a married couple, with two teenaged daughters and his parents living with them. In spite of these responsibilities, they served for months on end, often with just a few hours of sleep at night.

As the hospital began filling up with Covid patients who occupied all the beds and spilled out into the hallways, Dr. Amar felt some hesitation about working in such close proximity to infected people. He thought, "I don't want to catch the disease and bring it home to my family." In answer, he heard a voice within him say, "Would you hesitate to help your own children? These people are all your children!"

With this divine guidance, he served wholeheartedly throughout the pandemic. Both he and Dr. Mansi did contract Covid, but their children and parents were never infected.

Later in the pandemic, when the deaths began overwhelming even the crematoriums, Dr. Mansi was exhausted and hit an emotional wall. One day in particular she saw many deaths not only of the elderly, but also of young men who were the sole support of their families. She returned home in the evening exhausted and with a heavy heart. As she closed her eyes for a few minutes, she had a remarkable dream.

In it Master appeared in the hospital dressed in silvery-white robes, bustling here and there attending to the patients. He turned to her and said, "The disease is caused by bad karma brought on by people's negative thoughts. We can't stop the disease, but we must stay very busy trying to help everyone."

Mansi then began shaping balls of mud into babies. When she held them, they were living children; when she put them down they were only mud once more. "Don't you see?" Master said. "When Divine Mother touches them, they come alive. Otherwise they are dead. Don't grieve, my daughter." After this dream, Mansi was able to continue in her service.

So, my friends, in these stories you can see the beauty of living for God and serving Him in others. Our lives have been changed by witnessing such self-offering.

*With divine friendship,*
NAYASWAMI DEVI

# A LETTER TO GOD

Dear God,

This has been a particularly eventful year, and it seems fitting that I should write You a note of gratitude.

My heart is very full, and words seem insufficient. I know that You don't need my words of thanks any more than the sun needs to be praised for sending forth its rays, but for my own sake let me recognize how much love You shower on me.

First of all, thank you for this enlightened path and for the wonderful teachers You have sent. Let me thank You above all for Master and for Swamiji, who have molded my life and blessed my humble self-effort.

Thank you for Devi, my friend and life companion. What a joy and fulfilment our life together has been. And thank you for the joy that comes from our son and grandchildren.

Thank you, Divine Mother, for giving us so many loving friends. Everywhere we go You are wearing a different disguise, waiting for us with a warm smile and a new experience. Thanks, also, for the constant support and beautiful examples of discipleship with which you've surrounded us. What wonderful times we've had this last year: amazing food, interesting trips, and let's not forget all the jokes and laughter.

Thank you for the many outward gifts You have given us: of health, energy, and enthusiasm. I'm grateful, too, for having sufficient finances so that we not only have enough to live simply and comfortably, but also enough to share with others and to give back to You in remembrance that You are the giver of all that we have.

I'm grateful, too, for all the tests that You've provided. This year, with all the travel, has been particularly helpful in stripping away so many unnecessary necessities. The constant changes have helped me drop those unwanted habits that managed to creep in, and establish new and better ones instead.

But all these outward signs pale in comparison with Your inward gifts. Thank you for the peace of mind and the expansion of love that I feel when my mind begins to become still. Thank you for the inward yearning to reunite with You and for the techniques, especially Kriya, that bring me closer with each meditation.

Finally, thank you for the growing realization that it is all You. You are playing all the parts and doing all the deeds. It is, in a strange way, You writing this note of appreciation to Yourself. As "I" mentioned at the beginning, words seem insufficient.

*With deepest gratitude and appreciation,*
NAYASWAMI JYOTISH

P.S. This Thanksgiving has been particularly sweet, and writing this has been very fulfilling. You might want to write your own note of thanks to the Giver behind all gifts.

# THE MESSAGE IN A STRANGE ENCOUNTER

The winter's night was very cold and windy, and I huddled by the little stove in my camper reading the Bible by the light of a kerosene lamp. In the early years of Ananda our dwellings were simple — without electricity, running water, phones, or any way to communicate with others.

But we were more than happy to live in whatever was available — campers, teepees, old delivery trucks — just to be part of Ananda. Here we could dedicate our lives to God as well as help Swami Kriyananda fulfill Yoganandaji's dream of world brotherhood colonies.

On this particular night as I was reading, I was startled to hear a loud pounding on the door. I cautiously opened it, and there on the cinder block step stood a strange man with a wild look in his eyes.

"I need to come in," he said in a demanding voice. Offering silent prayers to God for protection, I stood aside and let him enter.

He sat down on one of the two benches at my little table. "I'm hungry. What do you have to eat?" he again demanded. (More silent prayers on my part.) I offered him some food which he ate voraciously.

"I'm thirsty. What can I drink?" (Still more silent prayers.) I placed some water before him, which he quickly gulped down.

Seeming to relax a bit he said, "I like it here. It's nice and warm." After a pause he added, "I have these big sores on my arms." He rolled up one of his sleeves and showed me open, oozing sores on his arm.

("Please God, resolve this quickly," I fervently prayed.)

A few more moments passed. Then he suddenly stood up and said, "Thank you. I have to go now," and quickly departed.

Totally baffled by what had just happened, I sat stunned for a few minutes. Then taking a few deep breaths, I continued reading the Bible. These were the first words that my eyes fell upon:

> For I was hungry, and ye gave me meat; I was thirsty, and ye gave me drink; I was a stranger, and ye took me in;

> Naked, and ye clothed me; I was sick, and ye visited me; I was in prison, and ye came unto me.

> Then shall the righteous answer him, saying, Lord, when saw we thee hungry, and fed thee? or thirsty, and gave thee drink? . . .

> And the King shall answer and say unto them, Verily I say unto you, Inasmuch as ye have done it unto one of the least of these my brethren, ye have done it unto me.

"God," I asked inwardly, "was it really You who came in the form of that desperate man?" I never saw the stranger again. To this day I've suspected that the encounter was God's way of showing me that He Himself receives any act of kindness we express to others.

Now as we approach the Christmas season, it's a good opportunity to introspect and cleanse our hearts of any negative emotions we may hold towards others. Throughout December, I'm taking up the personal challenge of holding only positive, loving thoughts towards everyone — be they wise or foolish;

well-kempt or disheveled. Remember that love offered to any form of life is love offered to God.

In *Whispers from Eternity*, Master writes: "Let every feeling that I have glow with Thy love. Let every act of my will be impregnated with Thy divine vitality. Let every thought, every expression, every ambition be ornamented by Thee."

I invite you to join me in this challenge for the rest of 2022: to feel God's love flowing through you in each moment of the day. This is the greatest gift you can give to the world. And who knows? God may come in hidden form to receive it.

*Your sister in God,*
NAYASWAMI DEVI

# DISCONTENT TO SOME EXTENT

D uring a recent talk in Bangalore, India, I said that most people are "discontent to some extent." Devi liked the catchy phrase so much that she even wryly suggested we should print it on T-shirts. Personally, I think that's going too far, but it does make a good topic for a blog.

Poetically speaking, God sings the universe into existence by chanting AUM, the vibration of duality. One of these dualities is likes and dislikes. As Sri Yukteswar put it, "The mere existence of a physical body signifies that its existence is made possible by unfulfilled desires." Poetically speaking, discontent is the glue that holds creation together.

One of the fastest (and happiest) paths to Self-realization is simply to accept things as they are. We spend so much time and effort pushing away things in the world that don't fit our particular bundle of likes and dislikes. Wanting things to be other than they are drains us of our energy.

Swami Kriyananda tells of an interesting revelation in this regard. This incident took place when he was living in San Francisco. His schedule was intense, with classes in different locations every evening as well as writing, correspondence, and counseling required during the day.

One evening he was scheduled to teach a class on "Energy and Energization" in Palo Alto, California. He stopped at his parents' house, which happened to be close to the classroom. His mother took one look at him and said, "You look exhausted. You just have to cancel that class tonight." He knew that wasn't possible, but compromised by taking a rest.

*I will willingly accept whatever is given to me as mine to do.*

Instead of falling asleep, he began to think of all the obligations that were sapping his strength. He realized that the problem wasn't the actual work itself but rather the energy drained by his mental resistance. One by one he visualized each obligation: the classes and commute time, the correspondence, the writing, the many people asking for his guidance. As each one arose, he deeply accepted it. As he did so his energy flooded back. When he emerged from the bedroom his mother remarked, "Oh, you look so much better! You must have had a good nap."

I was working with him at the time as his assistant, and he told me about the experience the next day. He concluded the story with a twinkle in his eye and the comment, "It was the best class on energy I have ever given."

This isn't just an interesting story but a life lesson. Who among us hasn't felt resentful about our responsibilities? And, who among us hasn't felt drained because of inner resistance? This very morning in meditation I was doing what Swamiji did that evening so many years ago. I was deeply accepting that which

God has given me to do. And, like Swamiji, I emerged from our meditation room with much greater energy and enthusiasm.

Let's use this holy advent season as a chance to develop new qualities and re-energize our spiritual life. Last week Devi wrote, "I invite you to join me in this challenge for the rest of 2022: to feel God's love flowing through you in each moment of the day. This is the greatest gift you can give to the world. And who knows? God may come in hidden form to receive it."

This week I invite you to add this challenge. From now until the end of the year practice this: "I will willingly accept whatever is given to me as mine to do."

If we do this we will become "more content to a great extent."

In joy,
NAYASWAMI JYOTISH

# FREEDOM IN FORGIVENESS

What is true freedom? Some would say, "It's the ability to do whatever you want whenever you want." That's certainly a kind of freedom, but it's one which ultimately leads to bondage. Living in that way, we become controlled by our desires.

There is another, more enduring, type of freedom. It comes through self-discipline, calming our mind, controlling our reactions to things, and accepting that everything in our life comes from God. This kind of freedom brings inner peace, and calm acceptance of whatever comes. Self-control frees us from sense compulsion, and from the ceaseless fluctuations of the restless mind. We become masters of ourselves.

Another key to finding inner freedom is the practice of forgiveness. We have no control over the behavior of others. Holding onto past hurts and grievances only strengthens the false thought that we are subject to the ceaseless fluctuations of an inimical universe. Forgiveness is an act of both divine courage and love. It affirms our strength, and our ability to react positively even in adversity.

"Yes," we may think, "I want to love everyone, but if you only

knew what she did to me—I just can't forgive her for that." With this kind of thinking, we reduce in our mind the vast field of God-awareness into mere patches of brambles and thorns. To forgive others reminds us that beyond the joys and sorrows of this world, our true life is in God.

In her book *The Hiding Place*, Corrie ten Boom tells a remarkable story of forgiveness. She, her father, and her sister Betsie were resistance workers against the Nazis in Holland during World War II. Though not themselves Jewish, they hid many Jews in their home and helped them to escape. Corrie and her family were eventually arrested and sent to a concentration camp, where her sister and father perished.

Corrie survived and later began a global ministry, sharing the teachings of Christ throughout the world. She tells this dramatic story:

> It was at a church service in Munich that I saw him, the former S.S. man who had stood guard at the shower door in the processing center at Ravensbrück. He was the first of our actual jailers that I had seen since that time. And suddenly it was all there—the roomful of mocking men, the heaps of clothing, Betsie's pain-blanched face.
>
> He came up to me as the church was emptying, beaming and bowing. "How grateful I am for your message, Fräulein," he said. "To think that, as you say, He has washed my sins away!"
>
> His hand was thrust out to shake mine. And I, who preached so often to the people in Bloemendaal the need to forgive, kept my hand at my side.
>
> Even as the angry, vengeful thoughts boiled through me, I saw the sin of them. Jesus Christ had died for this man;

was I going to ask for more? Lord Jesus, I prayed, forgive me and help me to forgive him.

I tried to smile, I struggled to raise my hand. I could not. I felt nothing, not the slightest spark of warmth or charity. And so again I breathed a silent prayer. Jesus, I cannot forgive him. Give me your forgiveness.

As I took his hand the most incredible thing happened. From my shoulder along my arm and through my hand a current seemed to pass from me to him, while into my heart sprang a love for this stranger that almost overwhelmed me.

And so I discovered that it is not on our forgiveness any more than on our goodness that the world's healing hinges, but on his. When he tells us to love our enemies, he gives, along with the command, the love itself.

The past two weeks, Jyotish and I offered you two practices to follow during this holy season: 1) to feel God's love flowing through you constantly throughout the day; and 2) to accept willingly whatever is given to you as yours to do.

Now in this third week of Advent—the month before Christmas—we offer you another suggestion. Follow these words of Swami Kriyananda: "Claim your soul's freedom! Bless all who ever harmed you, or ever wished you harm. Give them your love, and your prayer for their freedom in God."

May you, like Corrie, feel God's love flowing through you as you forgive others. May each one of us place our little candle on the divine altar of forgiveness, whose light can heal and bless the world.

*Wishing you blessings in this holy season,*
NAYASWAMI DEVI

# CHRISTMAS AND COURAGE

Courage is an essential quality, needed for success in both everyday life and spiritual growth. Fortunately, courage is an innate quality of the soul. We cannot avoid the challenges that come to us, because they are drawn by our own karma and the soul's longing to be free.

Paramhansa Yogananda says it this way: "Every day is a fresh opportunity on the part of the human ego to gather more and more exploits of heroism. Meet everybody and every circumstance on the battlefield of life with the courage of a hero and the smile of a conqueror. Whatever comes your way and needs attention must be considered a duty. Duty is not imposed upon man by any super-power. It is the inherent urge of life toward progression."

It is enlightening to contemplate the examples of great courage displayed in the lives of the great world saviors. Let's imagine, for a moment, the courage demonstrated in the story of Christmas.

Mary was an unmarried teenage woman in the small village of Nazareth when the angel Gabriel appeared to her and asked her to bear a holy child. Her first act of faith and courage was to say yes to this astounding request. *Whatever comes your way and needs attention must be considered a duty*.

Joseph, who was betrothed to Mary, had to have the courage to defy the cultural norms of the day and accept her. *Every day is a fresh opportunity on the part of the human ego to gather more and more exploits of heroism*.

Courage reveals itself through the *inner struggle* needed to say yes to whatever comes our way and needs attention. There are many other examples of valor shown by the young holy couple: the difficult circumstances of the birth in a manger, the visitations of angels and the three wise men, and the courage to flee to Egypt in order to save the young savior. As Yogananda puts it, *"It takes courage to renounce the known for the unknown."*

"Following the Star," by Nayaswami Jyotish.

In these last four "Advent blogs" we've given a few examples of spiritual qualities, especially courage: Devi's bravery in accepting a strange stranger into her home and giving him comfort, my challenge that we have the strength to "willingly accept whatever is mine to do," and Devi's challenge to have the resolve to forgive and "Bless all who ever harmed you, or ever wished you harm."

Here, then, is a final challenge for this year. Look into your heart and find something that has "come your way, needs attention, and must be considered a duty," but that you have been avoiding. Take on the challenge, face it head on, and conquer it, freeing yourself from its limiting cage.

During this holy season the Masters are supporting our efforts by sending powerful blessings of grace and courage. These are their Christmas presents to each of us, wrapped in joy and tied with the bow of love.

Devi and I also send you our loving thoughts and encouragement, that you may experience the Christ consciousness during this season and always.

Happy Christmas.

NAYASWAMI JYOTISH

# MAKING PERMANENT GAINS

A s we enter the new year, it's traditional to use this juncture as an opportunity to make resolutions about how we'd like to improve our life. It's a little discouraging, however, to think back on previous New Year's resolutions and realize that we'd resolved to change the same things in years past without any discernible results.

How much exercise equipment is bought at the beginning of the new year only to be sold unused a few months later? Yet at the same time, it's encouraging to reflect that we've never given up hope and are still trying. Our desire to improve remains with us, because it's prompted from a higher level of our own consciousness.

Once I was leading a New Year's retreat at The Expanding Light, during which we each made a list of resolutions for the coming year. During a break in the class, one of the students came up to me and said, "I find that very depressing."

"What do you mean?" I asked him in surprise.

"You've been on the spiritual path for a long time now," he replied, "and you still have things about yourself that you want to change?"

Fortunately a friend of mine, Roma, happened to be walking by at that moment and rescued me. With a twinkle in her eye, she said, "Devi is the only one in the community who isn't perfect yet. That's why we have her working with the guests." We all laughed, and I hope the young man realized that the search for perfection is a long process.

There's an aspect of personal transformation that's often over-looked, and it's the main thought I want to share with you today: To make lasting improvements in our life, it takes more than our own personal efforts. True inner change comes about through a combination of sincere devotion to God and the grace that it draws.

One of my favorite passages in the Bhagavad Gita is: "To those who meditate on Me as their very own, their hearts ever united to Me by incessant inward worship, I supply their deficiencies and make permanent their gains." (9:22)

It is God who "supplies our deficiencies." He/She alone knows our shortcomings, loves us unconditionally in spite of them, and gives us the strength and understanding to transcend them. Our minds may be clouded by past karmic tendencies, but when the light of God's love and wisdom shines in, we gain the power and clarity to overcome them.

And it is God who "makes permanent our gains." Sometimes it's hard to see the spiritual progress we've made. We can become so focused on how much farther we have still to go that we fail to appreciate how far we have already come. Remember, whatever progress we've made remains with us on some level, because it's based on the truth of our own being.

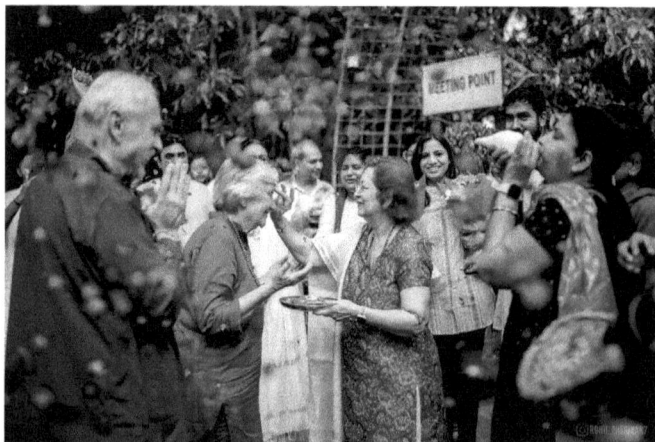

Through our devotion, the sense of "I-ness" that identifies with our limitations begins to dissolve. When, time and again, we stray from the knowledge of who we really are, God is there to steer us back on course towards our own highest potential.

So as we enter the new year, remember, whatever the outer circumstances, to keep your love for God foremost in your mind. This is the most powerful and effective way to turn our resolutions into realities.

Referring to the passage quoted earlier, Swami Kriyananda writes in *The Essence of the Bhagavad Gita: Explained by Paramhansa Yogananda*: "Thus, the highest teaching, which Krishna expounds here, is to love God, the Infinite Spirit, above all: 'to meditate on Him as one's very own.' God alone can lift us out of the relativities of karmic merits and demerits into the absolute peace and freedom of Infinite Being."

*Wishing you a blessed and joyful New Year,*
NAYASWAMI DEVI

# ABOUT *the* AUTHORS

**Nayaswami Jyotish and Nayaswami Devi** are disciples of the great master Paramhansa Yogananda (author of *Autobiography of a Yogi*) and students of Swami Kriyananda. Their mission is to help others live the teachings of Self-realization through meditation, devotion, and service.

Their lifelong dedication to the spiritual path has led them to lecture, teach, counsel, and serve throughout the world, spreading the message of peace through meditation.

They are recipients of the Global Ambassador Peace Award. This honor was conferred at the United Nations in a special ceremony by the Institute of International Social Development in recognition of their contribution to fostering world peace.

Since 1984 they have been the Spiritual Directors of Ananda Worldwide, pioneering Ananda's work in Italy and India and guiding the spiritual welfare of thousands of Yogananda's devotees. They are the co-authors of *Touch of Light, Touch of Joy, Touch of Love, Touch of Peace*, and *Touch of Divine Wisdom*. To see their schedule of appearances, lectures, classes, and events online and in person, go to **jyotishanddevi.org**.

**Nayaswami Jyotish** was named by Swami Kriyananda as his spiritual successor after decades of helping him build Ananda's work around the world. Jyotish began taking classes from Kriyananda in 1967. In 1969 they moved together to the foothills of the Sierra Nevada Mountains of California to found Ananda Village, a model spiritual community. Jyotish has also written several other books: *Lessons in Meditation, How to Meditate, 30-Day Essentials for Marriage,* and *30-Day Essentials for Career*.

**Nayaswami Devi** first met Swami Kriyananda in 1969 and dedicated her life to the spiritual path. She and Jyotish were married in 1975 and have spent their life together serving Swami Kriyananda and their guru, Paramhansa Yogananda. Devi is the author of *Faith Is My Armor: The Life of Swami Kriyananda,* and the editor of two of Swami Kriyananda's books: *Intuition for Starters* and *The Light of Superconsciousness*.

**jyotishanddevi.org**

# FURTHER EXPLORATIONS
# WITH CRYSTAL CLARITY

## CRYSTAL CLARITY PUBLISHERS

If you enjoyed this title, Crystal Clarity Publishers invites you to deepen your spiritual life through many additional resources based on the teachings of Paramhansa Yogananda. We offer books, e-books, audiobooks, yoga and meditation videos, and a wide variety of inspirational and relaxation music composed by Swami Kriyananda.

See a listing of books below, visit our secure website for a complete online catalog, or place an order for our products.

**crystalclarity.com**
800.424.1055 | clarity@crystalclarity.com
1123 Goodrich Blvd. | Commerce, CA 90022

## ANANDA WORLDWIDE

Crystal Clarity Publishers is the publishing house of Ananda, a worldwide spiritual movement founded by Swami Kriyananda, a direct disciple of Paramhansa Yogananda. Ananda offers resources and support for your spiritual journey through meditation instruction, webinars, online virtual community, email, and chat.

Ananda has more than 150 centers and meditation groups in over 45 countries, offering group guided meditations, classes and teacher training in meditation and yoga, and many other resources.

In addition, Ananda has developed eight residential communities in the US, Europe, and India. Spiritual communities are places where people live together in a spirit of cooperation and friendship, dedicated to a common goal. Spirituality is practiced in all areas of daily life: at school, at work, and in the home. Many Ananda communities offer internships during which one can stay and experience spiritual community firsthand.

For more information about Ananda communities or meditation groups near you, please visit **ananda.org** or call 530.478.7560.

# THE EXPANDING LIGHT RETREAT

The Expanding Light is the largest retreat center in the world to share exclusively the teachings of Paramhansa Yogananda. Situated in the Ananda Village community near Nevada City, California, the center offers the opportunity to experience spiritual life in a contemporary ashram setting. The varied, year-round schedule of classes and programs on yoga, meditation, and spiritual practice includes Karma Yoga, personal retreat, spiritual travel, and online learning. Large groups are welcome.

The Ananda School of Yoga & Meditation offers certified yoga, yoga therapist, spiritual counselor, and meditation teacher trainings.

The teaching staff has years of experience practicing Kriya Yoga meditation and all aspects of Paramhansa Yogananda's teachings. You may come for a relaxed personal renewal, participating in ongoing activities as much or as little as you wish. The serene mountain setting, supportive staff, and delicious vegetarian meals provide an ideal environment for a truly meaningful stay, be it a brief respite or an extended spiritual vacation.

For more information, please visit **expandinglight.org** or call 800.346.5350.

---

# ANANDA MEDITATION RETREAT

Set amidst seventy-two acres of beautiful meditation gardens and wild forest in Northern California's Sierra foothills, the Ananda Meditation Retreat is an ideal setting for a rejuvenating, inner experience.

The Meditation Retreat has been a place of deep meditation and sincere devotion for over fifty years. Long before that, the Native American Maidu tribe held this to be sacred land. The beauty and presence of the Divine are tangibly felt by all who visit here.

Studies show that being in nature and using techniques such as forest bathing can significantly reduce stress and blood pressure while strengthening your immune system, concentration, and level of happiness. The Meditation Retreat is the perfect place for quiet immersion in nature.

Plan a personal retreat, enjoy one of the guided retreats, or choose from a variety of programs led by the caring and joyful staff.

For more information or to place your reservation, please visit **meditationretreat.org**, email **meditationretreat@ananda.org**, or call 530.478.7557.

# Nayaswami Jyotish and Nayaswami Devi

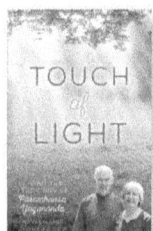

## Touch of Light

Living the Teachings of Paramhansa Yogananda
*Nayaswami Jyotish and Nayaswami Devi*

*Touch of Light* is taken from the popular blog entries of the same title. Like the facets of a beautiful diamond, each chapter's topic is a small reflection of the brilliance of one of the great spiritual figures of our time. Paramhansa Yogananda came to the West in 1920, bringing a new vision of how to live. He lectured across the United States drawing thousands, and filling the largest auditoriums. Since Yogananda's passing in 1952, his *Autobiography of a Yogi* has continued to inspire such influential people as George Harrison, Gene Roddenberry (creator of Star Trek), and Steve Jobs.

The authors were fortunate to have Kriyananda's training and friendship. With him they founded many of the Ananda communities. They know from experience that these teachings can improve all aspects of life: health, business, success, creativity, marriage, family, education, and spiritual development.

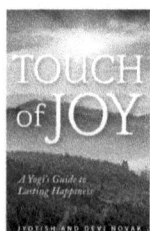

## Touch of Joy

A Yogi's Guide to Lasting Happiness
*Jyotish and Devi Novak*

Joy is an aspect of God, and is at the heart of our own soul nature. It is not to be found in outer fulfillments or gratifications, but exists without any cause. Swami Kriyananda, a direct disciple of Yogananda and spiritual teacher of the authors, once said, "Joy is the solution, not the reward." To learn to live with joy under all circumstances, and not to wait only until conditions are to our liking, is the secret of a happy life.

The authors are celebrated lecturers who have inspired many thousands around the world. They studied for nearly fifty years with Swami Kriyananda, and serve as Spiritual Directors of Ananda Worldwide. They live most of the year at Ananda Village, near Nevada City, California.

## Touch of Love

Living the Teachings of Paramhansa Yogananda
*Nayaswami Jyotish and Nayaswami Devi*

We, and the very fabric of the atoms, are made from love and joy, and our hearts will never rest until we are reunited with that reality," said author Nayaswami Jyotish. When we welcome the presence of love into our lives, our entire existence is born anew.

Once again, the authors accompany us on the journey of the heart: answering the call of true, unconditional love. This book is a compilation of weekly letters they posted in 2017 and 2018 to their popular blog, A Touch of Light. The letters are filled with spiritual teachings as practical as they are profound, faithfully shared in the spirit of their beloved guru, Paramhansa Yogananda, and his direct disciple, Swami Kriyananda.

## Touch of Peace

Living the Teachings of Paramhansa Yogananda
*Nayaswami Jyotish and Nayaswami Devi*

Tales of forgiveness, grace, challenge, and triumph will inspire and sustain the reader through every bend in the road of life. Each short chapter is an instructional jewel clarifying the nuances of such topics as: Dealing with Low Energy, Seeing Spirit Everywhere, Finding Calmness in the Midst of Activity, and How to Enjoy Long Meditations. In this book you will discover how to balance the inner life of meditation with the outer life of work.

## Touch of Divine Wisdom

Living the Teachings of Paramhansa Yogananda
*Nayaswami Jyotish and Nayaswami Devi*

In divine wisdom there is bliss absolute, bliss infinite, bliss eternal! This fifth installment follows the authors as they share the wisdom they have gained through over fifty years on the spiritual path. They offer the keys for how to live a happy, fulfilled life—no matter the challenges swirling around us these days—through the ancient yogic teachings of Paramhansa Yogananda. The authors share engaging and easy-to-read blogs such as: Dealing with Change and Loss, Hope for a Better World, Keeping Your Balance, and Faith, Attunement, and Courage.

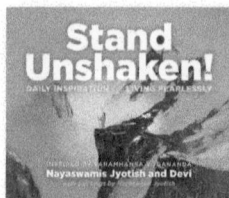

## Stand Unshaken!

Daily Inspiration for Living Fearlessly
*Nayaswami Jyotish and Nayaswami Devi*

"You must stand unshaken amidst the crash of breaking worlds!" It was Paramhansa Yogananda who issued this soul-stirring exhortation. How do we follow his great example and become warriors for the Light? *Stand Unshaken!* offers inspiration and practical guidance on how to live courageously during these turbulent times. Each secret of living fearlessly (one for each day of the month) is paired with a beautiful painting by Nayaswami Jyotish. Awaken within you the power to live in joy whatever your outward circumstances, stand unshaken, and become a true light unto the world.

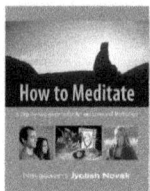

## How to Meditate

A Step-by-Step Guide to the Art and Science of Meditation
*Jyotish Novak*

This clear and concise guidebook contains everything you need to start your practice. With easy-to-follow instructions, meditation teacher Nayaswami Jyotish demystifies meditation, presenting the essential techniques so that you can quickly grasp them. Since it was first published in 1989, *How to Meditate* has helped thousands to establish a regular meditation routine. This newly revised edition includes a bonus chapter on scientific studies showing the benefits of meditation, plus all-new photographs and illustrations.

*"The clearest, most practical, and most inspiring guide on meditation I've ever read."* —**Joseph Bharat Cornell,** meditation instructor, author of *Sharing Nature*

## Faith Is My Armor

The Life of Swami Kriyananda
*Devi Novak*

The life of Swami Kriyananda is the story of a modern-day hero—a man who achieved extraordinary victories by demonstrating spiritual courage, determination amid great obstacles, and personal sacrifice.

*Faith Is My Armor* tells the complete story of his life: from his childhood in Rumania, to his desperate search for meaning in life, and to his training under his great guru, the Indian master, Paramhansa Yogananda.

## *The Original Writings of*
# Paramhansa Yogananda

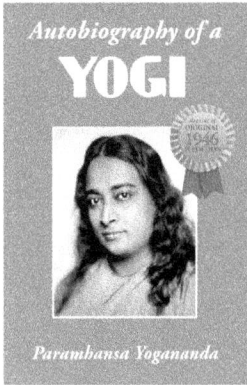

### THE ORIGINAL 1946 UNEDITED EDITION OF YOGANANDA'S SPIRITUAL MASTERPIECE

## Autobiography of a Yogi
*Paramhansa Yogananda*

*Autobiography of a Yogi* is one of the world's most acclaimed spiritual classics, with millions of copies sold. Named one of the Best 100 Spiritual Books of the twentieth century, this book helped launch and continues to inspire a spiritual awakening throughout the Western world.

Yogananda was the first yoga master of India whose mission brought him to settle and teach in the West. His firsthand account of his life experiences in India includes childhood revelations, stories of his visits to saints and masters, and long-secret teachings of yoga and Self-realization that he first made available to the Western reader.

This reprint of the original 1946 edition is free from textual changes made after Yogananda's passing in 1952. This updated edition includes bonus materials: the last chapter that Yogananda wrote in 1951, also without posthumous changes, the eulogy Yogananda wrote for Gandhi, and a new foreword and afterword by Swami Kriyananda, one of Yogananda's close, direct disciples.

## Scientific Healing Affirmations
*Paramhansa Yogananda*

Yogananda's 1924 classic, reprinted here, is a pioneering work in the fields of self-healing and self-transformation. He explains that words are crystallized thoughts and have life-changing power when spoken with conviction, concentration, willpower, and feeling. Yogananda offers far more than mere suggestions for achieving positive attitudes. He shows how to impregnate words with spiritual force to shift habitual thought patterns of the mind and create a new personal reality.

Added to this text are over fifty of Yogananda's well-loved "Short Affirmations," taken from issues of *East-West* and *Inner Culture* magazines from 1932 to 1942. This little book will be a treasured companion on the road to realizing your highest, divine potential.

## Metaphysical Meditations
*Paramhansa Yogananda*

*Metaphysical Meditations* is a classic collection of meditation techniques, visualizations, affirmations, and prayers from the great yoga master, Paramhansa Yogananda. The meditations given are of three types: those spoken to the individual consciousness, prayers or demands addressed to God, and affirmations that bring us closer to the Divine.

Select a passage that meets your specific need and speak each word slowly and purposefully until you become absorbed in its inner meaning. At the bedside, by the meditation seat, or while traveling—one can choose no better companion than *Metaphysical Meditations*.

## Songs of the Soul
*Paramhansa Yogananda*

**New Title Release: December 2023**
A Reprint of the original 1923 edition.

## ~The WISDOM of YOGANANDA~

This series features writings of Paramhansa Yogananda not available elsewhere—including many from his earliest years in America—in an approachable, easy-to-read format. The words of the Master are presented with minimal editing, to capture his expansive and compassionate wisdom, his sense of fun, and his practical guidance.

# Whispers from Eternity
*Paramhansa Yogananda*

*Edited by his disciple, Swami Kriyananda*

Many poetic works can inspire, but few, like this one, have the power to change your life. Yogananda was not only a spiritual master, but a master poet, whose verses revealed the hidden divine presence behind even everyday things. He felt that this book belonged among his chief literary contributions. As he wrote once in a poem, "When I am only a dream, Read my *Whispers from Eternity*; Eternally through it I will talk to you."

# Paramhansa Yogananda: A Biography

*With personal reflections and reminiscences by Swami Kriyananda*

Paramhansa Yogananda's classic *Autobiography of a Yogi* is more about the saints Yogananda met than about himself— in spite of the fact that Yogananda was much greater than many he described. One of Yogananda's closest direct disciples relates here the untold story of this great spiritual master and world teacher: his teenage miracles, his challenges in coming to America, his national lecture campaigns, his struggles to fulfill his world-changing mission amid incomprehension and painful betrayals, and his ultimate triumphant achievement. Kriyananda's subtle grasp of his guru's inner nature reveals Yogananda's many-sided greatness. Includes many never-before-published anecdotes.

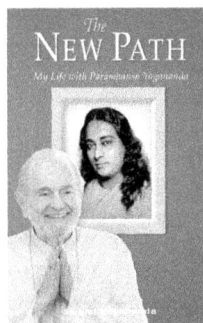

# The New Path

My Life with Paramhansa Yogananda
*Swami Kriyananda*

*Winner of the 2010 Eric Hoffer Award for Best Self-Help/Spiritual Book*
*Winner of the 2010 USA Book News Award for Best Spiritual Book*

This is the moving story of Kriyananda's years with Paramhansa Yogananda, India's emissary to the West and the first yoga master to spend the greater part of his life in America. When Swami Kriyananda discovered *Autobiography of a Yogi* in 1948, he was totally new to Eastern teachings. This is a great advantage to the Western reader, since Kriyananda walks us along the yogic path as he discovers it from the moment of his initiation as a disciple of Yogananda. With winning honesty, humor, and deep insight, he shares his journey on the spiritual path through personal stories and experiences.

Through more than four hundred stories of life with Yogananda, we tune in more deeply to this great master and to the teachings he brought to the West. This book is an ideal complement to *Autobiography of a Yogi.*

## The Essence of Self-Realization

The Wisdom of Paramhansa Yogananda
*Recorded, compiled, and edited by his disciple,*
*Swami Kriyananda*

Filled with lessons, stories, and jewels of wisdom that Paramhansa Yogananda shared only with his closest disciples, this volume is an invaluable guide to the spiritual life, carefully organized in twenty main topics.

Great teachers work through their students, and Yogananda was no exception. Swami Kriyananda comments, "After I'd been with him a year and a half, he began urging me to write down the things he was saying during informal conversations." Many of the three hundred sayings presented here are available nowhere else. This book and *Conversations with Yogananda* are must-reads for anyone wishing to know more about Yogananda's teachings and to absorb his wisdom.

*"Be assured that at each sitting, whether for one page or one chapter, you will have gleaned some refreshment for a tired heart or a thirsty soul. . . .* Essence *is easy to read, besides being quite a bit of fun."* —**Spirit of Change Magazine**

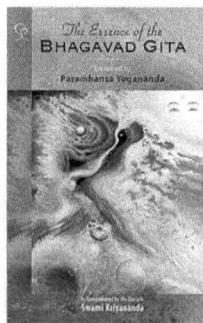

## The Essence of the Bhagavad Gita

Explained by Paramhansa Yogananda
*As remembered by his disciple, Swami Kriyananda*

Rarely in a lifetime does a new spiritual classic appear that has the power to change people's lives and transform future generations. This is such a book.

This revelation of India's best-loved scripture approaches it from a fresh perspective, showing its deep allegorical meaning and its down-to-earth practicality. The themes presented are universal: how to achieve victory in life in union with the Divine; how to prepare for life's "final exam," death, and what happens afterward; how to triumph over all pain and suffering.

*"It is doubtful that there has been a more important spiritual writing in the last fifty years than this soul-stirring, monumental work. What a gift! What a treasure!"* —**Neale Donald Walsch**, author of *Conversations with God*

## God as Divine Mother

Wisdom and Inspiration for Love and Acceptance
*Paramhansa Yogananda and Swami Kriyananda*

We long for a God who loves us exactly as we are, who doesn't judge us but rather helps and encourages us in achieving our highest potential. In this book, discover the teachings and inspirations on Divine Mother from Paramhansa Yogananda. These teachings are universal: No matter your religious background, or lack thereof, you will find these messages of love and acceptance resonating on a soul level. Included also are over thirty poems and prayers dedicated to God in the form of Divine Mother, and original chants and songs by the authors.

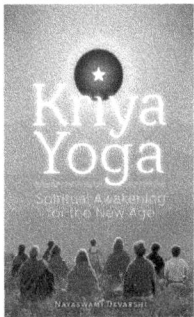

## Kriya Yoga

Spiritual Awakening for the New Age
*Nayaswami Devarshi*

Both instructive and inspiring, *Kriya Yoga: Spiritual Awakening for the New Age* is a roadmap for the already practicing Kriya Yogi. Through real-life stories from long-time Kriyabans, you will learn what attitudes and practices can help or hinder your progress on the spiritual path.

Simultaneously, this book is a signpost to the aspiring devotee on how and why to take up the lifelong practice of Kriya Yoga. You will discover what pitfalls to look out for along the way, and how to reach ultimate success on your journey to Self-realization.

## Once and Future Christ

Where East Meets West
*Nayaswami Hriman McGilloway*

There is a great need in these times for a deeper and more universal understanding of the teachings of Jesus Christ.

Paramhansa Yogananda came to America in 1920 to focus the light of India's timeless and timely wisdom upon the teachings of Jesus Christ. In *Once and Future Christ*, Nayaswami Hriman McGilloway expands upon that message with the inclusion of modern scientific discoveries and an exploration of the similarities and relationships between Christianity and yoga.

This book describes the inevitable evolution of Christian dogma towards greater inclusivity. The pathway of this future evolution leads to an understanding that the individual soul's relationship to God is the goal of the spiritual life.

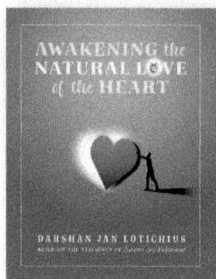

## Awakening the Natural Love of the Heart
*Darshan Jan Lotichius*

Swami Sri Yukteswar, the great yoga master and guru of Paramhansa Yogananda, speaks about the natural love of the heart and how it can be awakened. This process involves the removal of eight particular inner tensions, which he calls "the meannesses of the heart": hatred, shame, fear, grief, condemnation, racial prejudice, pride of pedigree, and lack of respectability.

With engaging candor, the author reveals the joy that blossoms as these "mean" traits in the heart are detected—and overcome. Whatever position you hold in society, wherever you are in your own soul search, these true-to-life stories and principles of spiritual psychology will help change your consciousness.

Following the clues given here, you can rise above depression, conquer oppressive tendencies, and reclaim the bliss of your own higher Self.